DOWIT'S
GABI

D1714341

STEVE HOLMSTROM

FOR MORE INFORMATION ABOUT
STEVE HOLMSTROM'S BOOKS & MINISTRY, OR
TO ACCESS HIS FREE VIDEO LIBRARY, VISIT:

OILPATCHPULPIT.COM

TABLE OF CONTENTS

To Dennis Wiedrick,

It only seems appropriate to dedicate this book to you. There is nothing in it I did not learn from you. Like most of my life messages, I heard you preach it first.

Being a spiritual son to you is something I love most about being me, and *Dowit's Gabi* is just one part of the rich inheritance I have received from you.

This one's for you Pops.

FORWARD

The kingdom of God is full of mysteries, as is the Bible and all of creation. While some are content to travel through life oblivious to these vast spiritual riches, others passionately give themselves to search out, understand, and employ them. Steve Holmstrom is one of these people.

For the twenty plus years I have known him, Steve has been on a relentless pursuit of kingdom truth. I cannot tell you how many times he has kept me up on some foreign mission field until 4 AM exploring the mysteries of the Bible!

The Bible says, *"Blessed are they who hunger and thirst after righteousness for they shall be filled!"* Steve's hunger has paid off. He has uncovered numerous valuable hidden treasures and unpacked these revelations through several outstanding books. This is another one of those great books!

Contained within the pages of this short volume is one of the greatest kingdom keys found in scripture, yet fewer than 10% of Christians understand this phenomenal truth. Many talk about it, some visit it on occasion, but few live it as a lifestyle.

With powerful testimonies and well-chosen scriptures, Steve captures our attention as he explains how God taught him these principles. This book will be a blessing to new believers, mature leaders, and even those exploring Christianity for the first time.

What is this amazing mystery? What is this secret which unlocks prisons and so many realms of the kingdom? I'm not going to tell you! I'm going to let you hear it in Steve's own words. What I will tell you, however, is this life-changing revelation can bring you into a union with Christ beyond anything you have ever experienced! Find out what Jesus really meant when he said *"I came that you might have life, and have it more abundantly!"*

Dennis Wiedrick

ONE

The Day I Left My Cage

It was a weeklong Pastor's Camp in August, 1999. I had heard remarkable things about this camp and was curious to see if the rumors were true. The speakers were said to be "apostles" and "prophets", titles new to me at the time. If there was even such a thing, I wondered what a modern day apostle or prophet might be like. How would they act? What would they say? I came somewhat suspicious and sceptical, yet excited to experience something new. To the spiritually bored, anything out of the ordinary is a welcome guest.

Dennis Wiedrick spoke the first night and I was spellbound. I'll never forget the way I felt as he shared. It was my first taste of renewal, a holy moment in my life. Dennis didn't talk like the denominational preachers I was used to. He was different. Firm and authoritative, yet without being bossy, he spoke of supernatural things matter-of-factly in a way that only one with experiential knowledge could. He led us through prayers of repentance in the middle of his message. He preached without notes and quoted scripture from memory continually. My heart burned within me as he opened the scriptures to us. From the moment I first heard Dennis speak I knew I wanted to walk with the man for the rest of my life.

When Dennis finished his message he invited people forward for ministry. I rushed to the front as fast as I could but it wasn't fast enough. Hundreds were already ahead of me. I wanted so much for Dennis to pray for me but with so many in front of me I began to doubt it was even possible.

Before Dennis prayed for a single person he scanned the crowd as though he was looking for someone in particular. To my amazement, he stopped searching the moment he spotted me! He stared at me for a few seconds, smiled, and began pushing his way through the dense crowd in my direction. I could hardly believe it. Was he actually pushing through to get to me? My heart pound with excitement. I felt like Zacchaeus, but taller. Five hundred sets of eyeballs watched Dennis stop immediately in front of me.

He turned off his microphone and said, "Young man, the Lord spoke to me concerning you. May I tell you what He said?" I assured him I was all ears. He continued, "The Lord showed me that you are living in a spiritual prison, like a bird in a cage. You take this prison with you everywhere you go and it is hindering your life and ministry. It is keeping you from getting close to others and keeping others from getting close to you. For you to go where God wants to take you, you absolutely must be freed from this prison." Though he was a perfect stranger, Dennis spoke as though he were my family doctor, completely convinced he knew me and what was best for me.

Dennis continued, "Now spiritually, I have to give you top marks. You love Jesus well. You spend a lot of time with Him and He visits you in your prison. But son, when it comes to the realm of your soul and how you relate to others I have to give you very low marks. You're not letting anybody in. No one knows you. No one gets close to you. You don't have a single friend. In fact, you don't even date."

Whether he was prophetic, psychic, or just a good guesser, the jury was still out, but I enjoyed the experience nonetheless. It was exhilarating to feel known, even for just a moment. He spoke so specifically, and so matter-of-factly, it was as though he had no fear of being wrong. I asked, "How do you know all this?"

Dennis didn't answer my question, but continued, "The reason you are living in this prison is because of the unforgiveness you have toward your father. He was never there for you and you have hated him for it. It is like you carry around with you a stack of I.O.U.'s for everything you believe he owes you. You cling to these debts he owes you, but unless you cancel them and tear them up you will live in this prison forever. If you want to have meaningful relationships in this life, you have to forgive your dad."

I thought we were just getting started, but Dennis smiled and said, "God bless you son," and then turned to minister to someone else. How could he be done? He had opened me up like a can of worms and then walked away and left me squirming. That was "day one" of the weeklong pastor's camp and I wandered around for days thinking about Dennis' words.

The next day at camp I signed up for a one-on-one meeting with a man named Tom, who everyone called a prophet. He took one look at me and said, "Why are you so afraid to fall in love?" It was a good question. Why was I so afraid to fall in love? What was it about being close to people that caused me such anxiety? Was it really a "spiritual prison?" Were there invisible bars surrounding me? Was that even possible? Or biblical?

The idea of "living in a spiritual prison" seemed like a weak excuse for being a loner. Wasn't it more likely I was just shy, unpopular, or unlikable? As unreasonable as it seemed, however, everything else Dennis said was true. I had no friends. No one really knew me. I didn't date. I didn't like being around people—at least not for very long. It was so bad, in fact, I had been living homeless for two months.

Let me explain that one. I had been renting a room with a house full of college guys but felt somewhat constricted by their presence. I didn't know why, but being around people made me uncomfortable. Even when alone in my room I found myself unnerved by hearing the others talking and moving about in the other rooms. Longing for silence and solitude, I purchased a new Gore-Tex bivy sac (an extremely small tent) and decided to try it out in the backyard. I enjoyed the peace and quiet so much that after a few weeks I cancelled my rent and began sleeping outside every night, usually in the trees beside one of the cities' golf courses. I kept my things in my car, cooked chunky soup over a camp stove, and showered at the church where I worked as a part time junior high youth pastor. I was a whole new level of loner. Even at the pastor's camp I chose to sleep in my bivy sac, alone in the middle of a field, rather than in the comfortable lodge with the other pastors.

Throughout the week my mind kept going back to what Dennis had said about my father. I knew it was true. I did hold a lot of unforgiveness toward him. He hadn't been there for me. He couldn't be. He died when I was only nine months old.

As a young boy, I held a high opinion of my father. My mother and grandparents often talked about what a great man of God Bernie Holmstrom was, a small town pastor who loved to lead worship with his guitar and share Christ with others. He had a special place in his heart for the First Nations people. The last church he pastored was in a hamlet called Kugluktuk (then called Coppermine), located north of the Arctic Circle on the Canadian mainland at the mouth of the Coppermine River. If you travel any further north, you're in the ocean. The cold one.

Bernie Holmstrom loved the outdoors, hunting, fishing, and riding his skidoo. In fact, that is how he died—or so I was told—in a skidoo accident. As a child I often wished he had survived to teach me those things. I only hoped I would grow up to be as much of an outdoorsman as my father.

That was my opinion of my dad until the day my older brother, Michael, decided to bring me up to speed concerning some circumstances surrounding his death. I was about eight years old when my brother said, "Steve, you still don't know how Dad died, do you?" I insisted I did, telling Mike he died in a skidoo accident because he wasn't wearing a helmet, and that's why we ought to always wear helmets when we ride. Mike said, "That's not how he died, Steve. I'll tell you how he died. He shot himself in the head with a gun!"

I didn't believe it for second. Mike found almost as much pleasure in causing me unnecessary grief as I did in causing him spankings by tattling on him for his endless harassments. I ran to my mother to rat him out, certain he would receive a glorious whipping for inventing such a gruesome fable. I could hardly wait to hear him squeal as the wooden spoon paddled his tail end. How could he say such an evil thing about my hero?

"Mom! Mom!" I cried, as I ran into her bedroom. "You'll never believe what Michael said! He said that you lied about dad's skidoo accident. He said dad shot himself in the head with a gun and killed himself!"

I watched my sweet mother turn pale. The look on her face told me there was something to my brother's story. "Sit down honey," she said nervously. I knew things were about to get real. Over the next ten minutes, as I sat on the edge of her bed, she explained to me how my father had been in a skidoo accident which resulted in major brain damage. For months he experienced agonizing pain and as a result he could hardly eat, sleep, or even think straight. It ruined his ability to preach, to sing, and to communicate clearly with others. Finally, lost in a cloud of depression and pain, he took his own life in our basement while my pregnant mother, my five-year old brother and I were upstairs. My brother heard the gun shot, a sound he would never forget.

As I listened to my mother's words I could feel something inside me shifting. The angelic like image I once held of my father was instantly obliterated. His halo vanished and was promptly replaced with feelings of embarrassment, distain and shame. My eight year old mind simply could not comprehend how anyone, for any reason, could do such a thing. A voice inside of me said, "So he didn't just die… he *chose* to die! He could have stayed if he were stronger or if he loved you more. But he wasn't and he didn't. He gave up. He couldn't take the pain. How selfish, how cold, how weak!"

For the next fifteen years I held unforgiveness toward a man I never knew. As I pondered Dennis' words, however, something inside of me began to soften. He was right. It was time to forgive my dad, to let it go, and to tear up those I.O.U.'s. But how?

There were more than a few. I would have never said it out loud because I knew it was too irrational to verbalize, but at some level I blamed my father for everything I hated about myself. As a child I failed at sports, but who is supposed to teach a boy how to throw a ball? That was his job. Beat up and bullied in elementary and junior high school, I blamed the absent father who never taught me to stand my ground. My inability to build a campfire, catch a fish, or shoot and gut a moose was his failure, not mine. I had an I.O.U. for every time Bernie Holmstrom failed to be what I thought I needed him to be. Where I was weak, he was to blame.

In my early teens, struggling with lustful thoughts and feeling a deep sense of guilt and shame, I longed for a father to talk to. I just wanted to know if I was normal or if there was something wrong with me. Why did I think about curvy women all the time, and how could I stop? I needed help. My mother had remarried, but my step dad wasn't the kind of guy I could talk to about personal things. He was a good provider and he loved my mom, but he didn't seem to like me. I figured if I told him what I was battling with he'd just call me a pervert. Desperate for answers, I finally went to my mother.

I said, "Mom, I've got a friend whose really struggling with lust and stuff but I don't know how to help him. I'm just wondering if there is a book or something on that subject?" My mother went to the Bible bookstore to search for *The Lust Book* but came back empty-handed. She told me she couldn't find anything on the subject and asked me if I wanted to talk to her about anything. I insisted I didn't and that my friend would be ok. In my heart, however, I wrote another I.O.U. to dad. Where was he when I needed him? Nowhere to be found.

Back to pastor's camp 1999…

Three days after my first encounter with Dennis, he spotted me as I was walking through the campground and called out, "Hey Steve! I was hoping to find you." I was amazed he remembered my name. He continued, "Tonight I am going to be preaching on the subject of spiritual prisons and if you're willing, I'd like you to help me by allowing me to minister to you publicly at the end. I want to teach these pastors how to set people free from spiritual prisons and I would like to have a live demonstration. Would you be my model?"

I wanted to say yes, even if only for the opportunity to have another moment with Dennis. My orphan heart melted with delight every time he was around. I saw in Dennis everything I ever wanted in a father, strength and influence, love and gentleness. Oh to have a dad like that! I wanted to please him by agreeing to be his volunteer, but certain I was beyond repair I feared his sermon might be ruined by his inability to help me. What would people think if he tried to fix me but couldn't?

I said, "I'm not sure if I'm your guy for this." He told me to think about it and to get back to him. By the time the evening service came around, I had talked myself into saying yes. While I didn't expect any real change, I couldn't pass up a moment with Dennis. Besides, I figured that even if he couldn't fix me, I could always pretend to be a little impacted in order to let him save face.

Before the evening service started, I found Dennis and told him I would do it. He already knew I would, but what he didn't know was the back story concerning my father. I told him about my father's suicide and a little more about my past. He asked for permission to share my story with the audience and I gave it to him. He assured me I would never be the same. I didn't believe him, but I enjoyed his excitement over me.

The Message That Changed Everything

Dennis preached on the subject of spiritual prisons by telling Jesus' parable of the unmerciful servant (Matthew 18:23-35). He called random people out of the audience and turned them into impromptu actors as he unpacked the story. It was quite amusing. One pastor played the part of the king. A few others were servants with debts which needed to be forgiven. Other people played tormentors who tormented those thrown in prison.

As the story goes, a king decided to settle accounts with his servants and he started with a fellow who owed him millions and millions of dollars (Dennis' version, but pretty close to the original). The servant was unable to come up with the cash so the king commanded he be sold, along with his wife and children and all he owned, in order to pay the debt. At this, the servant fell to the ground, begged for mercy, and promised to pay the debt if given more time. Fortunately for the servant, the king was moved with compassion and forgave his debt completely.

The servant was released and relieved to be debt free. On his way home, however, he spotted a fellow servant who owed him twenty dollars. He grabbed his fellow servant and started choking him (this was fun to watch people act out), saying, "Pay back what you owe me!" The fellow servant fell to the ground and begged for mercy, "Have patience with me and I will repay you." No mercy was given, and the man was thrown into prison to be tortured until the twenty dollar debt could be paid.

Those who witnessed the scenario reported it to the king who, now boiling with anger, called the first servant back in and said, "You wicked slave! I forgave you for millions of dollars' worth of debt because you begged for mercy, yet you couldn't forgive your fellow servant for a measly twenty bucks?" Furious, the king reinstated the multimillion dollar debt and handed the servant over to the torturers until he could pay back everything he owed.

To the delight of the audience, Dennis allowed "the tormentors" to have some fun tormenting the first slave in prison. When the laughter settled down, Dennis read Jesus' very sobering conclusion to the story, *"My heavenly Father will also do the same to you, if each of you does not forgive his brother from your heart."*

Dennis pointed out that two men were in prison due to one man's unforgiveness. He explained how unforgiveness imprisons us spiritually, which affects our lives in different ways. Tormentors, which are oppressive spirits, gain access to us when we hold unforgiveness toward others, and when others hold unforgiveness toward us. It was an awakening moment for many in the room that day. Few of us had realized how expensive it is to hold a grudge or to be in debt to another.

At this point Dennis said, "I would now like to invite my friend Steve up to help me". As I stood to my feet, five hundred people turned to see who Steve was. I could feel the temperature in my face rising as I walked to the front. He continued, "Now Steve has been living in a spiritual prison all his life…" He then, with me by his side, took a few minutes to explain how my father had taken his life, how that decision had impacted me, and how I had been holding unforgiveness all these years.

After bringing the audience up to speed he asked for two chairs to be brought on stage. They were placed side by side, but facing opposite directions. He had me sit in one while he sat in the other. The setup made it possible for him to hold me in a very long hug without having to stand. He asked me to put my arms around him, he put his arms around me, and two microphones were placed on stands directly in front of our mouths. By this time I was deeply regretting my decision to be his model! For a couple of grown men, the whole thing looked absolutely ridiculous.

Dennis said, "Steven, I know I'm not your father. I am, however, an intercessor, which is one who stands in the gap on behalf of another. Your father owes you an apology he is unable to give. Would you allow me to stand in the gap for him today and say some things on his behalf?" I acknowledged it would be alright, and he began by praying, "Father, I am asking as I stand in the gap for Steve's father, Bernie Holmstrom, that You would allow me to drink from Bernie's cup, to be touched by the feelings of his infirmities and of his weaknesses." At this, Dennis paused and took a few deep breaths, as though waiting for something before moving on.

He then continued, "Steven, I stand in the gap today for your biological father, Bernie Holmstrom, and on his behalf I want to say I am so sorry son, so incredibly sorry you had to walk life's road without me. God placed me in your life because you needed a father, yet I was never there. I see you as a little boy building with blocks alone in your room and oh how I wish I had been there to build blocks with you. Can you forgive me for not being there?"

All I could think about was the five hundred people staring at us and how ludicrous it all appeared. It felt like "playing house" in church, with Dennis playing the part of the daddy and myself the hurt little boy. I was dying a thousand deaths but because I knew it was too late to back out, I determined to do my best to forget the crowd and lean into the moment. In my mind I imagined myself taking the stack of I.O.U.s I held toward my father, finding one which said *"No Daddy to play with"* and ripping it up. With my fingers I even made the motion of tearing up a piece of paper as I awkwardly said into the microphone, "I forgive you… dad." When I heard my voice through the speakers I could not help but roll my eyes at myself. It sounded so outrageously cheesy I wanted to run away. Could this accomplish anything other than social suicide?

As though all was hunky dory, Dennis continued, "Thank you son. And as you grew, you needed a father to take you to the park, to throw a ball with you, to teach you to skate, to swim, and to ride a bike. You paid a big price in school, in sports, in friendships and in popularity because I wasn't there to help you win in these areas. I can't tell you how sorry I am. Son, can you ever forgive me?"

As I imagined myself tearing up another I.O.U., I said, "Yes dad. I forgive you." With my hands I made the motion of tearing up another slip of paper and imagined the pieces falling to the floor.

He thanked me and went on, "You've always felt poorly equipped when it came to the outdoors. I was a great hunter, but I never stuck around to teach you, my son, how to hunt, fish, build a campfire or set up a tent. Oh how I wish I had been able to enjoy the outdoors with you! Can you ever forgive me for robbing you of time spent in the wilderness with a father?"

By this time I was forgetting the crowd and things began to get real. With tears in my eyes I tore up another I.O.U. and said, "Yeah dad, I forgive you for that too. I won't hold it against you anymore."

He continued, "Son, as you matured into a young man you struggled in different ways and the enemy told you something was wrong with you. I should have been there to help you navigate that season of your life. You needed a father to remind you that you were a healthy young man, that everything was working properly, and to show you how to pursue a pure heart. Can you forgive me for not being there in that season as well?"

I imagined an I.O.U. which said *"The Lust Book,"* tore it up, and said, "I forgive you for that too dad."

Offence after offence, in no rush at all, Dennis repented to me for the things I had lost by losing a father. Some things he had knowledge of and other things just came to him in the moment. While I knew it wasn't truly my dad talking, it seemed to help my heart to hear a father acknowledging the pain I had suffered and asking for forgiveness. With every torn I.O.U. I felt lighter and lighter. My hard heart softened with compassion toward my father as I let go of each offence. I began to once again see the good in him I had long forgotten.

I thought we were finished when Dennis made one last request on behalf of my father. Saving the worst for last, he said, "Son, I know this won't be easy for you, but I have to ask you to forgive me for the way I abandoned your mother. I deserted my young bride when she needed me most. Can you ever forgive me for the pain, the difficulty, and the awful predicament I left your mother in?

My body tensed at the thought of it. This was the biggest I.O.U. of all and my knee-jerk reaction was to say no. I could forgive him for hurting me, but how could I forgive him for hurting my sweet mother? She was the most magnificent woman I had ever known, a true saint if there ever was one. How could he leave her to care for two little boys by herself? And pregnant too. She had to bring my little sister into this world all alone. What kind of a husband does that to a woman? I couldn't forgive him for that! Or could I?

I stared at that last I.O.U. and wondered if it was even possible to let it go. After some time, an awkward pause in our session, a voice inside of me seemed to say, "What are you gaining by holding onto this? It's time to leave this prison behind." And with that, I took a deep breath, tore it up and said, "I forgive you dad."

Dennis hugged me tighter and thanked me, on behalf of my father, for the generous gift of forgiveness. He then pulled back from the embrace we had been in for about fifteen minutes, of which I had my head on his right shoulder. He then had me place my head on his left shoulder which required an even bigger hug as I was now reaching over him completely, chest to chest, with our arms around each other.

In this new position he said, "NOW I want to speak to you from your REAL Father, your Heavenly Father, and I want to tell you I have *never* left you and I have *never* forsaken you! You were never alone because I was always there. You have seen Me through the lens of your earthly father, but I'm not like him at all. I never fail. I have never missed a moment of your life. When you thought you played alone in your room as a little boy, I was building blocks with you and I have always enjoyed the work of your hands. When you were downcast from your struggles in life, I was the One who lifted your head. You have often felt like no one knows you, notices you, or loves you, but I have always known you, I have always loved you, and I have never looked away. And I am so proud of you, My son, for the way you chose to forgive your earthly father. This is a big day for you and I. Our relationship can now go to a whole new place! I will be the One who is Fathering you from now on. For you truly *are* My son, and in *you* I am well pleased!"

I couldn't help but weep as the love of the Father flooded my heart. It was bliss. I knew in that moment, beyond any shadow of a doubt, I was accepted and loved by God. He was my Father, my true Father, and He would never leave my side. Something had changed. Something had lifted. Something had broken open and my heart was free! Just moments before, I had squirmed at the idea of hugging Dennis publicly, but now I didn't want to let go.

As we stood up from our chairs I once again became aware of the crowd who had been watching us, but it didn't matter anymore. People were sobbing all over the room, some weeping bitterly. I saw Kleenex boxes being passed down the aisles. Dennis smiled at me and said, "Well son, how do you feel?"

I said, "I feel like I'm in a cloud of... daddy!" It sounded dumb, but it was the perfect word. Daddy. If "daddy" could be an atmosphere, I was in it. I finally knew what it felt like to be a son, loved and accepted by a Father. The orphan was gone. I would no longer walk alone. I had a Father. The best Father of all.

As I walked toward my seat a man in the front row stepped in front of me, hugged me, and began to weep. He was a stranger to me and though I had not been a hugger in the past, something had apparently changed. I quite enjoyed hugging this fellow. I did not know him, but I loved him. When he let go, a woman hugged me as well, which was also quite nice. After that, someone else grabbed me, and then another, and another. By the time I left the building it seemed I had hugged half the room—and I loved every minute of it. The prison which had once held me captive had been unlocked. I was now free to love and to be loved.

Late that evening I went for a walk on the beach under a brilliant starry sky, trying to wrap my mind around what had happened. Like one who suddenly and unexpectedly inherited a great fortune, I considered my future and how things might change. As I walked barefoot in the cool sand I became acutely aware that God was walking with me. I was not alone. "Dad?" I said, "What does this mean for me? Will this feeling inside of me actually last? Will You stay this close? Will You really Father me?" He didn't answer, but I knew the answer. He had always been with me and would always be with me. I had to learn to stop shutting Him out.

The next week, back home in Edmonton, I experienced an unusual grace as I spoke to our youth group on the subject of the Father's love. It seemed as though my Father was loving His other children through me. At the end of my message I asked if anyone wanted prayer. Nikki, an adorable thirteen year old girl, darted to the front and buried her face in my chest, hugging me tightly before melting into a puddle of tears. By the time she let go of me, almost every teen in the room stood behind her in a line. None of them wanted prayer. They all wanted to be hugged. One by one I held them in my arms, allowing the Father to love each one through me. By the time I was finished there were teens laying all over the floor. Some were crying. Some were sleeping. Some sat staring at me with a look that seemed to say, "What happened to Pastor Steve?" I left the meeting that night bursting with the Father's love and hugged another dozen people in the parking lot. When I ran out of people I actually hugged a light pole. It was a little cold.

That was over two decades ago and I still hug everything that moves and a few things that don't. There was nothing gradual about the change that occurred in my life. It was as instantaneous as *"I was blind but now I see"*. People I had never been able to connect with in the past immediately found me approachable. My old boss, Graydon, who had once wanted to fire me over my cold and distant ways, immediately became my closest friend. I soon started dating, fell in love, got married, had five kids and fell in love with them too. I have now enjoyed two decades of rich friendships and intimate relationships. I walked out of that old prison and its steel gates have remained unlocked ever since.

It took Dennis all of about fifteen minutes to completely free me from a life behind bars, and he did it without praying a single prayer. Instead, he chose the ancient path of *intercession*. Before we talk about the difference between prayer and intercession, I need to tell you one more story.

TWO
Dowit's Gabi

A few months after meeting Dennis I moved to Ethiopia to work with Brian and Val Rutten, Canadian missionaries who had been serving in Africa for decades. I had just completed my third year of a four year Bible School degree but decided not to finish. School disagreed with me, or perhaps I disagreed with school. I wrote to Brian, saying, "I will do anything. I'll clean toilets, you name it, just let me come to Africa!" Brian and Val not only offered me the guest room in their basement, but also set up ministry opportunities for me in Ethiopian Bible Schools and churches. It was my first trip to Africa and I was certain my preaching would singlehandedly turn the continent upside down for Christ. The only question was how many days it would take.

On my first night in Ethiopia, while praying on my knees, the Lord spoke to me and said, *"I don't want you preach or teach at all right now, I brought you here to be an intercessor."* While I knew it was the Lord, I wrestled with the word all night. What did He mean? What would that even look like? And what would Brian and

Val say if I turned down the ministry opportunities they set up for me? Would they ask me to leave? Intercession wasn't what I came for.

The next morning at breakfast I told Brian and Val what I believed God had said. It was an awkward conversation. I felt stupid trying to explain it because it didn't even make sense to me. If I wanted to intercede for Ethiopia, I could have done it from Canada. Why come all the way to Africa just to pray? Fortunately, Brian and Val were gracious. Brian looked at me and said, "Steve, I don't understand all there is to intercession but I have seen the power of it and I thank God for intercessors. Just do what God is telling you to do." The ministry they had planned for me was cancelled and I headed to the basement to do God-knows-what.

How does an intercessor spend his days? I figured if intercession was my full time job, I ought to spend at least three or four hours a day in prayer, so I determined to do at least that. It wasn't easy. I had never prayed a solid hour in my life, never mind three, and moving to Africa did not magically transform me into a passionate prayer warrior. I was still an easily distracted twenty-three year old with a tendency to daydream. Praying fervently for hours, or even feebly for that matter, was not my forte. I didn't even know what to pray for.

I asked the Lord to save the lost souls of Ethiopia, but there was no fire on it. Just words. I prayed for the churches there and its leaders. I prayed for Brian and

Val and their mission work. Most of all, I asked God to give me something more useful to do! After I had prayed for everything I could think of I looked at the clock only to be crushed with disappointment. Only four minutes had passed! I still had two hours and fifty-six minutes to go.

For weeks I fell asleep on my knees, then woke up, apologized and drifted off again. If I wasn't sleeping I was daydreaming. Attempting to stay focussed, I tried praying out loud, but eventually my words drifted off and I would catch myself having conversations in my head about things completely unrelated to prayer.

Since meeting Dennis and Katie I had been reading a book by Norman Grubb titled *Reese Howells Intercessor*. Reese's sacrificial lifestyle and the odd ways in which he identified with those he interceded for inspired me to no end. I wanted to be an intercessor like Reese Howells and Dennis Wiedrick, one who changed lives through intercession. That was the life for me! Or so I thought. It was all so inspiring until I actually tried to do it. There in my basement suite in Ethiopia, as I struggled to stay awake in prayer day after day and hour after hour, the life of intercession quickly lost its sparkle. Maybe, I thought, it just wasn't for me.

Each day, after my three hours of pathetic prayer, I would go for a walk through the city of Addis Ababa. Being a tall white man made me a target for beggars, but I didn't mind. Before heading out I would fill my pocket with a hundred small coins. Each one was sufficient enough to provide a hungry soul a meal to eat. As I meandered through the city children ran up beside me crying out, "Father! Father! I'm hungry!" It was often all the English they knew, but more than enough to get a donation from me. Surprised at how quickly I would reach into my pocket for a coin, the children would dart off, only to re-emerge with a few pals who also received a prize just for showing up.

The aroma of fresh bread filled the streets at the same time each evening around a local bakery just as the hot rolls were coming out of the oven. I couldn't help but stop, and as I would leave the bakery with two large bags full of hot rolls, the street kids would scurry out of the shadows to meet me. I always started with thirty to forty rolls but rarely got to eat one. By the time I reached my home the little ones (and the not so little ones) had cleaned me out. I once tried to hide the last roll in my inside pocket for myself. But alas, a homeless princess in a tattered flower dress came out of the shadows, batted her pretty brown eyes, and I had no strength to deny. I got a hug, and she got my last roll.

Dowit

One man, more than any other, stands out in my memory. His name was Dowit. He looked like a beggar, but he never begged. I would pass him a few times each day on my walks because he lived on the side of the road about a block from where I was staying. His "home" was a depressed looking lean-to he had created out of a beat up brown tarp full of holes propped up by a couple sticks.

Dowit was a shy fellow, but always wore a smile. The years had taken a toll on his right knee and as a result he walked with a limp. About fifty years old, he was slim, short, nearly bald, and possessed a body odor uniquely his own. His dark skin was dusty and dry from living rough under the open sky. Dirty beyond description, it seemed to me if I were to wring out the grungy rags Dowit called clothes, disease would drip in liquid form. The holes in his pant legs were so large his knobby knees and most of his emaciated legs popped out whenever he crouched down, which was his favorite position. Yet despite his limping, stinking, dirty, tattered and sun scorched demeaner, Dowit's eyes sparkled with a goodness that made him beautiful. I couldn't help but like him, warts and all.

I always stopped to give Dowit some change and whenever I did he looked at me with an expression that seemed to say, "Oh, you shouldn't have!" Something about the little man won my heart. I sat with him on the side of the road for five to ten minutes each day, attempting to make conversation. It wasn't easy. His English was weak and my Amharic was non-existent. Eventually we discovered a few dozen English words he knew and we kept our dialogue around them. Sometimes I'd show up with a couple bottles of cold Coke, or a little food, and we would share a meal together on the curb. People would stare as they passed by, curious as to why the rich white guy was so chummy with the street bum. We ignored them, talked about nothing, and sipped our Cokes. I could tell Dowit enjoyed our visits, as quiet as they were.

On Christmas day of 1999 I spent the entire evening with Dowit on the side of the road. Over his tiny campfire, in a pot full of red sauce he had prepared, he cooked me the spiciest chicken ever consumed by mortal men. Later that evening I fell asleep by Dowit's fire. While I slept he covered me with his own blanket.

One morning, during my prayer time, the Lord spoke to me and said, "I want you to intercede for Dowit." Still somewhat believing intercession to be just another name for prayer, I said, "Sure Lord, I'll start praying for Dowit." And I did. I prayed that he would come to know Christ. I also prayed God would heal Dowit's knee so he could get a job and get off the streets.

A few days after my commitment to intercede for Dowit, while sitting with him at his usual spot, we were approached by a gabi salesman. A gabi is a traditional Ethiopian blanket made of white cotton with decorative stitching around the edges. It is common to see their older men and women wearing a gabi much like we wear a jacket. It is worn over their clothing, covering the upper body. Some cover their head with it as well, like a hoodie. The gabi man, who had a sack full of these blankets, stood in front of me displaying his treasures.

I turned to Dowit and asked him if he wanted one. With an enthusiasm I did not expect over such a small gift, Dowit insisted he would love a gabi. I bought it for him and he wasted no time putting it on. He wrapped it around himself, pulled it over the top of his bald head, and tightened it against his dark cheeks. His face, peeking out from the bright white cotton, beamed like a delighted baby cozy in his beloved blankie. I had never seen Dowit so happy. I was actually taken back by it. Why all this excitement over a boring white blanket?

I knew Dowit liked the gabi, but I didn't realize just how much he liked it until the next day when I passed him on the road and saw him wearing his gabi—but *only* his gabi. He had taken off all his filthy rags and, except for the gabi, Dowit was buck naked. Fortunately it covered the necessities, but just barely. He was wearing the gabi so high his skinny legs were almost completely exposed. I laughed and said, "Dowit! You're naked, you silly man! You look like a chicken. Put some clothes on brother!"

He giggled and said, "It nice! It nice! So good!"

As I considered Dowit's usual outfit, I understood his logic. His clothes were disgusting. I often found my skin itching immediately after one of our visits. I would always hug Dowit before leaving, and then the scratching would begin. Genuinely concerned about catching fleas, I was quick to go straight home and scrub with soap. How he wore those filthy rags, and if they had ever been washed, was beyond me. That gabi was the only clean thing he owned. I could understand why he wanted to feel that fresh soft clean cotton right against his skin. For a man who almost never felt clean, this new gabi was a little heaven on earth.

I assumed he would be back in his clothes the next day, but he wasn't. Nor the next day or the day after that. In fact, for weeks I would pass him on my daily walks and jokingly shout out, "Hey naked man! Put some clothes on!" All he wore for the next month was his new gabi. The only thing that changed was its color.

With the exception of a decorative blue, black, red and yellow strip of embroidering around the outer edge, Dowit's gabi was bright white when I gave it to him. It didn't take long, however, for it to lose its luster. He wore it all day and slept in it all night. He spilled food on it when he ate, and cheap alcohol when he drank. Because Dowit made a small fire each evening to cook and keep warm on the side of the road, smoke and ashes and dirt and grunge soon filled Dowit's gabi. Before long it looked and smelled just like everything else he owned. His prized blanket had become a filthy and tattered rag.

About this time I decided to purchase a new gabi for myself. I intended to use it as a prayer blanket. I had, for a few months, been praying under a blanket. This began after an experience I had the day I left Canada to fly to Ethiopia. On that day I met a woman named Barbara Simmons, a worship leader from Ontario, who was awoken early in the morning with a song from the Lord. He told her to sing it over a man she would meet that day. Dennis was driving me to the airport but made an unexpected stop at a friend's house to drop something off. Barbara, his friend's daughter, was at his house and when she saw me she instantly knew I was the man she was to sing over.

Barbara walked toward me with a blanket and asked me to kneel on the floor. It was an odd request from a stranger, but I went with it. She put the blanket over me and began to sing the song of the Lord, which came from Psalm 46. Tingles ran up and down my spine as she sang, *"God is my refuge… God is my refuge… God is my refuge and strength… A very present help when I'm in trouble… God is my refuge, I will not be afraid."* From that day forward I had been wearing a blanket during my prayer times. I often wore it over my head much like the Ethiopians wear a gabi. I decided to purchase a new gabi I could use during prayer.

Because I hadn't seen the gabi salesman for several weeks, I mentioned my desire to purchase a gabi to an Ethiopian woman named Tirunesh. She worked for Brian and Val in their ministry office which was beside my basement suite. She told me she knew of a shop where she could purchase a high quality gabi for me, but suggested I not come with her as the price would only increase with a white guy in the room. I gave her the money and Tirunesh delivered the gabi the next day. It was beautiful, much nicer than the one I had bought for Dowit. This one had gold embroidering around the edges and the thousands of threads surrounding the outer edge had been twisted by hand to create a thousand little braids. The cotton itself had a luxurious feel to it. I could hardly wait to pray in it.

I headed home and went straight to my room, immediately wrapping myself in the new gabi. As I began to pray I clearly heard the Spirit say to me, *"Take that thing off. I don't want you praying in that."*

I paused for a moment, wondering if perhaps what I heard was my imagination, and then continued in prayer. He immediately spoke again, but firmer, *"Take that thing off! I don't want you praying in that!"*

"But Lord," I persisted, "It is the nicest gabi money can buy. It's my new prayer blanket. I bought it for You!"

I tried to continue to pray once more, but He said a third time, *"Take that thing off! I don't want you praying in that."* It made no sense at the time, but I tossed it aside and continued gabi-less.

Later that day, while out on my walk, the Holy Spirit spoke to me just as I was passing Dowit on the road. He said, *"I want you to trade gabis with Dowit today."* I rolled my eyes and laughed out loud, suddenly realizing why He wouldn't let me wear it. It was never meant to be mine.

This wasn't the first time God asked me to give my stuff to Dowit. A month earlier, by the word of the Lord, I had given Dowit a very expensive sleeping bag I had brought with me from Canada. I had complained at the idea of giving it away, telling the Lord a sleeping bag of that quality was not meant to lie on the hard ground. But God said, *"That's why I want you to give him your Thermarest mattress as well."* I argued again, saying it would be stolen if he went anywhere, and he couldn't possibly walk around with a sleeping bag and a Thermarest under his arms, but the Lord said, *"That's why I want you to give him your backpack too."* It was a thousand dollars' worth of brand name camping gear, but I eventually gave in. I showed up one evening as Dowit was building a fire to stay warm. I told him he wouldn't need a fire anymore, and helped him set up his new bed. He seemed to like it, but he didn't have it long. I never asked whether it was stolen or sold. He used it for a few weeks and then it was gone.

I decided to go easy this time. I said, "Sure Lord, I'll give Dowit my new gabi." It wasn't a big deal anyway, a heck of a lot cheaper than all the camping gear I gave him. Besides, I figured, I could just go buy myself another one.

I immediately heard the same voice inside me say, *"I didn't say 'give'. I said 'trade'. I want you to trade gabis with Dowit today."*

Trade? I laughed and said, "Lord, why on earth would I want a filthy, disgusting, stinky, disease covered gabi like that one for? I wouldn't put that rag on my worst enemy! No Lord! I'll give him the new one and he can keep the old one too. He can have both."

The Lord spoke once again, *"You'll do it."*

I took a longer walk that day, turning the idea over in my mind for hours. It made no sense. Was this God or was I just talking to myself and looking for ways to be weird? Was my mind playing tricks on me? What would I do with a smelly old rag like that anyway? I had no clue, but being eighty percent sure I had heard the Lord, I didn't want to risk being disobedient. I decided to make the trade and figured I could toss the old one in the garbage later.

After arriving home from my walk I grabbed the new gabi, wrapped it around myself and headed to Dowit's place. Just for fun, I even put it over my head like the locals do. I was going to enjoy it for a least a few minutes before I had to give it away. I expected Dowit to laugh at the sight of me in a gabi, but he didn't. He just froze and stared. Then, after a moment, he looked down at his own filthy gabi, and then back at mine. I could see he was embarrassed, and I felt stupid for causing him shame. Perhaps he hadn't yet realized how dirty his gabi had become, but in stark comparison to mine, his looked like trash.

I said, "Hey Dowit, do you like my new gabi?"

He said, "It nice. It good one".

I said, "Well I'm glad you like it, cause I want to trade gabis with you today." His look told me he didn't understand, so I spoke slower and made motions with my hands, saying "I want to trade my gabi for your gabi. You give me yours and I'll give you mine."

This time he understood and immediately opposed the idea, saying, "No Steve. It good one.

Good one for you." Then, pointing to his own gabi he said, "This good nuf' for me." I insisted, and then he insisted again. He did not want to trade. The conversation went back and forth a few times until I nearly shouted, *"Dowit! I want to!"* Oddly enough, and I couldn't imagine why, I actually *did* want to. Something in my heart had shifted in the moment. I knew Dowit needed the clean one, and that I somehow needed the dirty one.

By this time a small crowd had gathered to watch, which was not unusual. People seemed to find it amusing that I spent so much time with the little homeless man. They would often stop and stare at us as we ate our food or sipped a Coke. We certainly were an odd couple.

With an audience watching, Dowit conceded to my trade but was in no way supportive of it. Since I was the only one with clothes underneath, I removed my gabi first and wrapped it around his. Then I said, "Now you give me yours." With a bit of a sigh, Dowit slipped off the dirty gabi from underneath the clean one and handed it to me through the layers, trying not to reveal his nakedness. Then, to Dowit's horror, I took the filthy gabi he had been wearing and wrapped it around myself, over my head, and tight around my face just as Dowit had worn it. He burst into tears and cried, "No Steve! Take off! Take off! That not good for you!"

By this point my spirit man had risen up and was clearly taking charge of the situation. I seemed to be waiting to see what he—my spirit—would do next. I heard myself say, "It's ok Dowit. I want to!" Then I hugged him, kissed him on his bald head, and walked away wearing Dowit's gabi.

Arriving at home, I immediately went to my room to pray. Oddly, I felt compelled to be as close to Dowit's gabi as possible and so—alone in my room— I took off my clothes, knelt on the floor, and covered myself completely with the dirty gabi. I don't exactly know how to explain what happened next, but in an instant I was drenched in what seemed to be *the person of Dowit*, if that makes any sense. All I could smell was Dowit. All I could see was Dowit. All I could feel was Dowit—his pain, his loneliness, his shame, his oppression, his addictions, his demons, his misery. It was as though, for a few minutes, I became Dowit.

Until this moment I never understood what Dennis meant when he said intercession was "more than just praying for someone," but rather "standing in the gap and taking their place". He often referred to "drinking their cup" in order to be touched by the "feelings of their infirmities". In this moment, however, I realized exactly what Dennis meant. It was as if I had crawled into Dowit's skin in order to pray the prayers he was unable or unwilling to pray.

I was finally Dowit's intercessor, standing in his place, but what would I pray? I determined to ask God to heal Dowit's knee, to change Dowit's life, and to save Dowit's soul. But when I opened my mouth to pray I heard myself shout out, *"Oh God! Please heal MY* knee! Jesus change MY life! Lord save MY soul! I need you Jesus! I need you Lord! Save ME! Wash ME! Cleanse ME! Heal ME! Forgive ME! Rescue ME! Set ME free!" Then suddenly, like a woman in labor, a groan that came from deep in my abdomen exploded out of my spirit like a gusher and I groaned until I had no breath left to groan. With that, I collapsed exhausted on the floor under Dowit's gabi, dazed and wondering what the heck had happened. (Dennis hadn't mentioned anything about boys pushing out babies in the prayer room!)

The next day, as I walked down the road, Dowit saw me from a distance and ran toward me jabbering excitedly in Amharic while slapping his right leg. Eventually, remembering I only spoke English, he switched and said, *"Me knee! Me knee! No pain all day! Me knee all good!"* I was as shocked as he was. My prayer actually worked, and he didn't even know I had prayed for him. I said, *"Dowit! I prayed for your knee just yesterday! Jesus healed you!"*

Later that day, arriving home, I entered the compound where I was staying and was stopped by Tirunesh, the woman who had purchased the new gabi for me. She was visibly shaken up as she pulled me aside and said, "Steven, I have to tell you something! Yesterday I saw you leave here wearing that beautiful new gabi I got for you."

I said, "Yeah, but about that gabi…"

She interrupted and said through tears, "Well while I was walking home I passed you on the road.

You didn't see me, but I saw you, and by that time you were wearing that filthy, smelly, disgusting gabi that homeless man has been wearing!"

"That was me," I said.

Her tears now literally sprayed from her eyes as she sobbed, "Steven, I have been working for Christian organizations for years, and I have been surrounded by Christians my whole life, yet I have never surrendered my life to Jesus. But yesterday when I saw you in that dirty gabi, I looked right at your face but…" She then wept aloud and tried again, "But I couldn't see your face! I knew it was you, Steve, but it wasn't you! I saw JESUS! With my eyes! I saw Jesus! And I went home and cried half the night. He came to me and I gave my life to Jesus last night. I'm a Christian today! I'm a Christian!"

I begged her to tell me if she was exaggerating in the least, but she insisted she was not. I wondered if it could be true. Like, truly true? Did Tirunesh actually see the face of Jesus Christ? In me? Her tears seemed to say so. Her face beamed with joy, excitement, and newness of life. She certainly looked like a woman who had just seen God. How wonderful, I thought, to think God used my intercession to impact not only Dowit, but Tirunesh as well. I couldn't have planned it if I tried.

A few days later I asked Tirunesh to accompany me to visit Dowit. I wanted to share the gospel with him. I had witnessed to him in the past through an interpreter but he had been unwilling to surrender to the Lord. With Tirunesh's help I shared the gospel with him again. This time he said, "That's what I need! Yes! Yes! Jesus I need!" The three of us knelt together on the side of the road as Dowit gave his life to the Lord.

Within a week, Dowit vanished. I asked around but no one knew where he had gone. He never even said good bye. He had lived in that same spot on the side of the road for years, yet within days of his salvation he disappeared. Why, I wondered, would he ever leave that spot? Everybody knew him there. They liked him. He was like part of the street. People showed him kindness every day. It didn't make sense to start over somewhere else.

Whether Dowit got a job, moved, died, or grew wings and flew away, I do not know. One day I'll ask him.

"Those who make the practice of intercession a part of their lifestyle will grow toward a life as unoffendable as the life of Jesus. As you come to the throne of grace on behalf of another, sincerely and humbly, you step into their shoes. You cannot walk in someone else's shoes and not grow in mercy and forgiveness. This has all the potential to keep you free of offence, which empowers your prayer life."

Katie Wiedrick

THREE

A Lesson on Intercession

I searched for a man among them who would build up the wall and stand in the gap before Me for the land, so that I would not destroy it; but I found no one (Ezekiel 22:30)

The Bible tells us God searches for intercessors, for those who will stand in the gap. But why? Why does God need intercessors? In fact, why does He need anyone at all? He's God! What does our intercession give Him that He doesn't already have? Or any type of prayer, for that matter? If God knows what we will pray before we pray it, why do we need to pray at all?

The very idea of prayer and intercession seems ludicrous until you understand *authority*, who has it and who doesn't. Like many revelations, this one begins in Genesis chapter one. Verse twenty six says:

> *Then God said, "Let Us make man in Our image, according to Our likeness; and let them rule…"*

God gave rulership over the earth to humans. The word *rule* in this passage means to *dominate*, or *to have dominion*. Simply put, man is in charge. That doesn't mean we own the world. *The earth is the LORD'S, and all it contains, the world, and those who dwell in it* (Ps. 24:1). God is most certainly the owner. There is a big difference, however, between ownership and rulership. God may own it, but we are in charge. And if we are in charge, God is not.

This used to confuse me until I heard Dennis Wiedrick explain it. He said, "Think of it like leasing a home. Leasing a home doesn't make you the owner, but it does leave you in charge. *You* mow the lawn. *You* vacuum the floors. If you make a mess, *you* are the one who cleans it up. For all intents and purposes, it's yours. You don't expect your landlord to pop by every day and mop your floors. In fact, once you've signed your lease, the owner has no legal right to step inside *unless you invite him*. He can't just waltz in anytime he wants and act like he owns the place, even though he does. It would be trespassing for him to enter, and it's the same way with God."

God is no trespasser. Jesus will not barge into your life uninvited and start fixing things. He *stands at the door and knocks* (Rev. 3:20). Talk about respecting boundaries! The God who created the world *knocks before entering*. If we choose to hear His voice and open the door, He comes in. If we don't, He won't.

God honors the authority He gave to men. Even when Adam chose to surrender that authority to the devil through sin, God respected his choice. For a season, Satan became *the ruler of this world* (Jn. 14:30). Authority had been *handed over to him* (Lk. 4:6). While God wasn't willing to leave the world in such a miserable condition, He also wasn't willing to trespass the authority he gave to men. What could He do? There was only one legal way to fix the problem. God had to *become a man* and take the authority back from the devil *as a man.*

Enter Jesus. He lived a righteous life because anything less would cost him the authority He inherited by being born a man. He then died on a cross and paid the price for our sins in order to strip the devil of the authority we lost because of sin. Once all authority in heaven and earth had been handed over to Jesus, He turned around and gave it right back to men. From that day until this, anyone who repents of their sin is washed in the blood of His sacrifice and the devil is disarmed of authority over that person's life. Thank God for His blood!

It is important to note that Satan does not have unrestrained power and authority to use against us. The devil needs our agreement and cooperation. The primary ways we cooperate with him is by believing his lies, agreeing with him, or by choosing to sin. Yes, sin matters! In fact, few realize how serious it is. Unrepented sin gives the devil a legal right to mess with our lives, destroy our relationships, our families, our finances, our cities and our nations. The reason the ruling spirits over your city have the authority they do is because of the unconfessed sins of the people. Unconfessed sin is a wide open door to the enemy.

This is why repentance is so important. It is why Jesus, John the Baptist, and all the disciples preached the same sermon: *"Repent, for the kingdom of heaven is at hand!"* If the kingdom is what you are after, repentance is the starting point. It strips the devil of his authority and unlocks kingdom power. Without repentance, however, we are stuck in the enemy's grip. Jesus said, *"Unless you repent, you will all likewise perish"* (Lk. 13:3).

When someone is unwilling or unable to repent, God searches for an intercessor to do it for them

But what if a person doesn't understand the importance of repentance? What if they are unwilling to repent, or convinced they have done nothing wrong? Or what if they think all this Jesus stuff is hogwash, nonsense and gibberish? Ahhhh… that's where the intercessors come in! When someone is unwilling or unable to repent, God searches for an intercessor to do it for them.

Repenting For Someone Else

I was stopped in an airport recently by a couple who had heard me speak at a conference. After a little chitchat the woman said, "Steve, we heard you preach on intercession and we loved your stories, but to be honest, we've wrestled with whether or not 'repenting on behalf of someone else' is scriptural. It just seems so strange. Where is that in the Bible?" It wasn't the first time I had been asked the question and it is something I once wondered myself. I was convinced intercession worked, because it changed my life so dramatically, but at first I didn't know where to find it in the Word.

It was the same for Dennis and Katie at the beginning. A man named Jack Winter ministered to them, it deeply impacted their lives, and as a result they began to intercede for others. Miracles happened whenever they did, but at first they wondered if all this "praying as someone else" was spiritually legal. Dennis would say to Katie, "I don't know what we're in, but it's working!" Being a Word man, Dennis began to dig, and was glad to discover intercession is most certainly biblical. For the remainder of this chapter we will unpack a biblical foundation for intercession.

Two Types of Intercession

In the first two chapters I shared two personal experiences. They illustrate the two distinct types of intercession: *horizontal intercession* and *vertical intercession*. The story of Dennis' intercession for my father is an example of *horizontal intercession*, the act of one individual standing in the gap in repentance on behalf of another individual *to a person*. Its human to human, on a horizontal plain. The story of Dowit's gabi is an example of *vertical intercession*, the act of one individual standing in the gap in repentance on behalf of another individual *before God*. It is human to God, on a vertical plain. Horizontal intercession and vertical intercession are two separate prayer tools. Let's look at them one at a time.

1. Horizontal Intercession

Maybe you're thinking, "Why repent to men? Men can't forgive sins!" Oh but we can, and we must. Jesus said, *"If you forgive the sins of any, their sins have been forgiven them; if you retain the sins of any, they have been retained"* (Jn. 20:23). Many have used this scripture in an attempt to prove the necessity of confession to priests, but it has nothing to do with saving souls or avoiding eternal punishment. We forgive people their sins not to change their eternal destiny, but to change their present destiny. It is about setting people free from the prisons holding them captive, the prisons keeping them from emotional, relational, and even financial prosperity.

Horizontal intercession is tremendously helpful. Perhaps I could have forgiven my father without Dennis standing in his place, but it hadn't happened yet. I was stuck. At the time, I didn't even recognize I held any unforgiveness, nor what my unforgiveness was costing me. Clueless to my prison, I had assumed my lonely and solitary lifestyle was due to being insecure and unpopular. I didn't know freedom was even an option. Dennis' intercession created for me a pathway to healing, smooth and easily attainable. I may have lived my whole life as a lonely soul hiding in solitude, as many do, but Dennis gave me the gift of horizontal intercession and I was set free from my prison in an instant.

It may seem strange to some, this "repenting as though you are someone else", but horizontal intercession is one of the greatest gifts you can ever give. It does for our generation what John the Baptist did for his. Concerning John, the book of Luke says:

> *"The voice of one crying in the wilderness, 'Make ready the way of the Lord, make His paths straight. Every ravine will be filled, and every mountain and hill will be brought low; the crooked will become straight, and the rough roads smooth; and all flesh will see the salvation of God.'"* (Luke 3:4-6)

How do we make a straight and smooth path for the Lord in the lives of those we intercede for? We do it by repenting of the high places in their lives, as well as the low places and the crooked places. When we repent of things like pride, *the mountains are brought low.* When we repent of self-hatred the *ravines are filled.* When we repent of twisted thinking, sexual immorality, or wayward living, the *crooked places become straight.* Through our intercession we make *the rough roads smooth; and all flesh will see the salvation of God.*

If the Holy Spirit gives you a burden for someone bound by unforgiveness, help them get unstuck. Tell them you are an intercessor, explain what an intercessor is, and ask for permission to stand in the gap for the one who hurt them. Repent to them, as Dennis repented on behalf of my father. Give them the gift of intercession. They may be a young Joseph with a destiny to rule the nation, but stuck in a prison you could unlock in a matter of minutes.

I once met an exotic dancer on a plane who wanted nothing to do with Christianity because she believed it to be led by oppressive and domineering men who only wanted to crush and keep women down. Rather than disagreeing, or attempting to prove I was different, I said to her, "I want to ask you, on behalf of male Christian leaders, if you would forgive us for the way we have misrepresented Jesus Christ? Jesus knew how to love and honor a woman, but we have often failed in that department miserably! Please forgive us for the way we have oppressed women. Please forgive us for not recognizing that God promised to pour out His Spirit on both men and women. I'm so sorry we have often treated women as second class citizens. That is not God's way." As I sincerely confessed the sins of domineering male leadership I watched this beautiful young woman's heart soften before my very eyes. As a result, we were able to have a wonderful conversation about the Lord. She is very near the kingdom of God.

It is especially important to watch for those with "father wounds". While we ought to forgive everyone, it is particularly important to forgive the father figures in our lives because a person's image of God is often distorted by the weakness they see in their fathers, step-fathers, or even spiritual fathers. If your dad was angry, you'll see God as angry. If your dad was cheap, you'll see God as cheap. If your dad was too busy for you, that's how you'll see God. By forgiving our fathers the lens through which we see God becomes clear and He is able to reveal Himself as He truly is, a perfect, tender, loving, generous, and merciful Father.

If you would like to dive deeper into the revelation of the Father's love, read Jack Winter's book, *The Homecoming*. You can also find some of his messages online. He was a pioneer in restoring the long lost message of the Father's love and horizontal intercession to the church.

2. Vertical Intercession

While horizontal intercession deals with sins committed against men, vertical intercession deals with sins committed against God. Do you know someone who needs to repent to God but is unwilling? Do it for them! Yes, you are allowed. No, it won't get them to heaven, but it will bring the kingdom of heaven to within their reach.

This is what Stephen was doing in Acts chapter seven when he cried out, *"Lord, do not hold this sin against them!"* Think about that for a second. Stephen was being stoned to death, yet his top priority was his murderers' forgiveness. How selfless. That's an intercessor. So much like Jesus, who prayed the same thing concerning his killers, *"Father, forgive them; for they do not know what they are doing."*

When a spirit of intercession comes upon a person, their heart's cry is for the forgiveness of others and (depending on the intensity) some intercessors will do just about anything to obtain it. The Apostle Paul's intercessory burden for Israel was so intense he said, *"For I could wish that I myself were accursed, separated from Christ for the sake of my brethren, my kinsmen according to the flesh"*. Paul was willing to go to hell to purchase heaven for Israel. It wasn't an option for him, but it does reveal his intercessory heart. He was willing to take their place at any cost.

That is what intercession is all about—taking someone else's place. It is about doing something someone else doesn't know to do, want to do, or is too stuck to do. It is more than simply "praying for people". In *A Royal Priesthood*, Dennis Wiedrick writes:

> In this hour, it has become popular to use the label of "intercession" to cover all kinds of prayer. But intercession by its very definition always involves "standing in the gap on behalf of another."

We see the spirit of intercession clearly upon the prophet Daniel in the prayer he prays in Daniel chapter nine. Over and over he confesses the sins of his people, but rather than saying "they" have sinned, he continually includes himself in the equation by using the word "we". Though he hadn't been one of the transgressors, he prays as though he had.

> **We have sinned**, *committed iniquity, acted wickedly and rebelled, even turning aside from Your commandments and ordinances. Moreover,* **we have not listened** *to Your servants the prophets... Righteousness belongs to You, O Lord, but* **to us open shame**... *because* **we**

have sinned against You… *we have rebelled* against Him; nor have we obeyed the voice of the LORD our God, to walk in His teachings… so **the curse has been poured out on us**… for **we have sinned** against Him… **we have not sought the favor of the LORD** our God by turning from our iniquity and giving attention to Your truth… **we have not obeyed His voice… we have sinned, we have been wicked… because of our sins and the iniquities of our fathers**, Jerusalem and Your people have become a reproach to all those around us…

(Daniel 9:5-16, emphasis mine)

When did Daniel sin, commit iniquity, act wickedly, or rebel? When did he neglect the words of the prophets? When did he stop seeking God's favor? Daniel was a man who sought God's favor even when it landed him in a lion's den. He had done none of those things. So why did he pray his prayer so self-inclusively? Why add "we" to every statement? It is called *identificational repentance*. Yes, it's biblical.

Identificational Repentance

Identificational repentance is when we step forward to confess the sins of our family, business, church, city or nation—or anyone other than ourselves. It is the overflow of this type of prayer which has preceded every significant move of God in history. Personally, I have seen more immediate transformational miracles through this type of prayer than any other.

We see identification repentance not only in the life of Daniel, but in many of God's prophetic people. Jeremiah modelled it when he prayed, *"**We** know our wickedness, O Lord, the iniquity of our fathers, for **we** have sinned against You"* (Jer. 14:20). Jeremiah wasn't wicked. He chose the word "we" because this was not a prayer of petition, it was a prayer of intercession.

Nehemiah did the same thing:

> *Let Your ear now be attentive and Your eyes open to hear the prayer of Your servant which **I am praying** before You now, day and night, **on behalf of the sons of Israel**... **We have acted very corruptly** against You and have not kept the commandments, nor the statutes, nor the ordinances which You commanded Your servant Moses* (Neh. 1:6-7, emphasis mine)

Notice Nehemiah starts by saying, *"I am praying... on behalf of the sons of Israel."* He is praying in their stead. In their place. He is standing in the gap. That is identificational repentance. That is intercession. It is the kind of prayer which precedes revivals, shakes nations, and stops the judgement of God. God looks for those who will *stand in the gap* for others, but true intercessors are often hard to find.

> *"I searched for a man among them who would build up the wall and **stand in the gap** before Me for the land, so that I would not destroy it; but I found no one"* (Ez. 22:30).

God searches for intercessors because destruction is inevitable where there is a lack of intercession. Will you be an intercessor? Not just one who prays, but one who stands on behalf of another? For families? For businesses? For cities? For nations?

When Your Feelings Don't Belong to You

Perhaps you are saying, "I'm in, but where do I start? How do I decide who to intercede for? Do I just pick whoever I want and start repenting as though I am them?" No. Intercessors do not run around standing in the gap for anyone and everyone. At least the mature ones don't. Our intercessory assignments are to be directed by the Holy Spirit. As a rule, I don't carry burdens He's not putting on me, and I don't drink cups He's not handing to me. We are to be led by the Spirit. You will often hear mature intercessors quote the following passage.

> *In the same way the Spirit also helps our weakness; for* **we do not know how to pray as we should**, *but the* **Spirit Himself intercedes** *for us with groanings too deep for words (Rom. 8:26, emphasis mine).*

We, in our humanness, confess we do not know what or who to intercede for, but the Holy Spirit does. When we come to Him and ask for direction, He reveals to us the burden He wants us to carry, the gabi He wants us to put on. Remember, God is *looking* for intercessors. If you tell Him you are available for intercession, He will gladly give you an assignment.

Very few are applying for this job so you are certain to be hired! Join with other intercessors and wait upon the Lord until He moves you *with groanings too deep for words.*

What are these groanings, you ask? For lack of better words... feelings. They are stirrings and responses within our spirits that prompt us to act. It can come as a burden, a heavy weight, something that doesn't sit right, or just an inner knowing that something has to change about a certain situation.

Now please don't hear what I'm not saying. I'm not saying we are to allow feelings to control us. I am saying, however, intercessors need to pay careful attention to their feelings because it is through feelings Holy Spirit often reveals intercessory assignments. This is why intercessors often say, "I'm feeling this..." or "I'm seeing a picture of that..." or "My gut is telling me..." or "I'm sensing...". Intercessors pay attention to feelings.

One of the most anointed intercessors I've had the privilege of knowing is a woman who has become a mother to me, Katie Wiedrick. I cannot imagine where my life would be without her intercession. For certain I would have lost both my ministry and my marriage. Only God knows how many times she has put on my size 13s, stood in my shoes, and repented for me when I was too thick headed to do it myself. I'm not telling you those stories in this book, but I will tell you that whenever Katie stands in the gap for me, *something always happens* and I'm a richer man because of it.

If you ask Katie how she knows what to intercede for and when, she will talk to you about feelings. She pays careful attention to her feelings, especially those uncommon to her. Uncommon feelings are often a dead giveaway the Holy Spirit is leading you in intercession for someone else. He's offering you their burden to bear and their cup to drink, allowing you taste what they are experiencing. He's handing you their dirty gabi.

> **Uncommon feelings are often a dead giveaway the Holy Spirit is leading you in intercession for someone else**

When Katie was new to intercession she did not understand the spiritual exchange of emotions involved, and thought she was going crazy. In *A Royal Priesthood*, Dennis tells a story about a time Katie became overwhelmed with an emotion she couldn't understand. When Dennis finally got her to express what she was feeling, she said, "I just feel like I don't want to be married anymore! I'm tired of being a mother! I can't put up with these kids! I hate this house! I hate my life! I just want to pack up and leave!"

Now you would have to know Katie to know how unlike Katie those words were. She's the exact opposite. She is an amazing wife and mother, full of love, and nothing makes her happier than being at home with family. When I come over and "let" her cook for me, she thinks I'm doing her a favor! Those feelings didn't belong to her.

Then Dennis said, "Katie, I believe you have picked up someone else's burden. I believe God is allowing you to feel what somebody else is feeling. Perhaps you're experiencing this so you can stand in the gap for them." Katie instantly remembered her friend Linda was feeling exactly like that. Relieved to discover her negative emotions were not her own, Katie stood in the gap for Linda that day in repentance before God. It went something like this:

"Father, I come to you on behalf of Linda, and as Linda, I want to confess that I don't love my husband anymore. I have lost the desire to be a mother to my children, and I feel like running away. Forgive me Father for the hopelessness I have allowed to permeate my whole life. I choose now to repent and turn back to you, and say 'yes' to your plan for my life."

Immediately the burden lifted, all the negative emotions were gone, and Katie was herself again. On top of that, she received a phone call from Linda the very next day at 2 p.m. She was calling to let Katie know she had an unexplained miracle in her life. She told her she had come to the place where she didn't want to be married any longer, had run out of grace for her kids, and had been about ready to pack her bags and leave. "Then yesterday," she said, "I don't know why, but God came to me, and suddenly I realized how wrong it would be to do this. It was as if I woke up from a bad dream. And now I realize that I love my husband! I love my kids! I enjoy my life! Isn't that wonderful Katie?" Katie never told her about the cup she drank on Linda's behalf.

Feelings and intercession go hand in hand. In *The Happy Intercessor*, Beni Johnson writes:

> "For many years, I did not know that I was an intercessor. When I look back now, I can see all the signs: I spent so much time carrying so many feelings inside of me and internalizing them as if they were my own."

When you have feelings uncommon to you, pay close attention to them. They may not belong to you. When you have dreams where you do things you would never do, pay attention to them. The Holy Spirit may be trying to speak to you. He may be allowing you to be touched by someone else's burden for the purpose of intercession. Once you've done the intercession, the burden will lift and grace will be released to them.

It was the intercessor in the Apostle Paul who wrote:

> *Now I rejoice in* **what I am suffering for you**, *and I fill up* **in my flesh** *what is still lacking in regard to Christ's afflictions, for the sake of his body, which is the church* (Col. 1:24 NIV, emphasis mine).

That's an intercessor for you. *"I am suffering for you!"* Are you willing to suffer for someone else? Will you allow your prayer life to go so far as to touch your flesh? Will you allow yourself to be touched with the feelings of someone else's infirmities? Will you wear their dirty gabi?

> *For we do not have a high priest who cannot* **sympathize with our weaknesses,** *but One who has been tempted in all things as we are, yet without sin* (Heb 4:15 emphasis mine).

This scripture tells us Jesus *sympathizes with our weaknesses.* He feels our stuff. Or as the King James Version puts it, *He is touched with the feeling of our infirmities.* How wonderful to have a God who takes our place. Consider the most despicable and nauseating temptations you have ever faced, and the shame you felt when you succumbed to those temptations, and remember that Jesus volunteered to *feel what you feel* and was *tempted with what you are tempted with.* Why would a Holy God do something so gross? Because love doesn't put on rubber gloves before it touches you. Love crawls into your muddy pit, kisses you on the lips, tells you you're beautiful, and carries you out of your mess. Love's not afraid to get dirty. Neither are intercessors. It's what we do.

Love's not afraid to get dirty. Neither are intercessors. It's what we do.

Jesus is the ultimate example, the Granddaddy of intercessors. If you want to see intercession at its finest, just look to the cross. Our sin, the transgression of mankind, was the filthiest gabi the universe has ever known, yet Jesus took it upon Himself. He took our place. *He was pierced for our transgressions. He was crushed for our iniquities. The chastening for our well-being fell upon Him, and by His stripes we are healed.* He did that for you and I. That was His cross to bear. Now what about yours?

> *If anyone wishes to come after Me, he must deny himself, and take up his cross and follow Me* (Matt. 16:24)

If you wish to go after Jesus you must carry a cross as well. If His cross meant wearing someone else's dirty gabi, shouldn't your cross include the same? Intercession isn't neat and tidy, sometimes it's as ugly as hell, but it is the way of the Master. You never look more like Jesus than when you take upon yourself someone else's filthy mess in order to get it off their back.

What If I'm Not A Feeler?

You might be asking, "But what if I don't feel anything?" I've been there. There have been many times I have engaged in intercession without a whole lot of feelings and experienced incredible results nonetheless. One of my greatest intercessory assignments (next chapter) was quite void of feelings and yet it led to an immediate and powerful miracle.

So no, feelings aren't everything, but they do matter and ought not be ignored.

It may sound like asking for trouble, but I encourage you to invite the Holy Spirit to allow you to be *touched by the feelings* of those you intercede for. It is a painful privilege and an agonizing honour to feel what they feel, to drink their cup, to taste their hurt, their pain, and their shame. When I put on Dowit's gabi, I put on the worst of Dowit, but it was an indescribable honour. It was the key to unlocking his prison and Dowit didn't have a chance of staying the same.

FOUR

I Love You Too

Big Ben, as he was often called, was a bear of a man who came from Danish descent. Being six-foot-four and over three hundred pounds, Ben Andersen was almost always the largest man in the room. With giant hands, a burly chest, broad shoulders and a deep voice, he intimidated many. To a toddler, however, the man was larger than life. Ben married my mom when I was three years old and we had a love-hate relationship from the beginning. I loved him and I was pretty sure he hated me.

Ben came across to many as gruff. He wasn't mean, he was too quiet to be mean. He just seemed a bit grumpy most of the time. Raised in poverty by a mother and father who were about as cuddly as a couple of honey badgers, he came by crustiness honestly. When my mother married him she was astonished to discover his family did not show physical affection of any kind. Ben didn't even hug his own mother.

I knew from the start that he wasn't my "real dad". That was always clear. To my mother's chagrin he didn't act like my dad, and my grandparents were always quick to remind me he wasn't. "You're a Holmstrom," they insisted, "not an Andersen!" They loved to tell me stories about the wonderful father I never knew. They weren't being helpful, but they meant well. They missed their son and wanted me to be proud of my name.

In my heart, however, I wanted to be an Andersen. I wanted to be big and strong like Ben. My mother told me he was planning to officially adopt my brother and my sister and I, and when he did we would become Andersens too. Oh how I dreamed of becoming Steve Andersen! That, I believed, would change everything. He'd be my dad, I'd be his son, and we'd go camping and fishing and hunting and who knows what else. It was a magnificent dream, but it never materialized. He never got around to filling out the paperwork—nor the camping, fishing, or hunting.

It is amazing what kids will do to earn love. As a small boy I would carefully comb through the coins in my mother's purse searching for "horse quarters", the 1973 Canadian quarter which displayed a Mountie on his horse. Ben collected horse quarters, he had a whole jar full of them, and every time I found one for him it seemed as though he liked me a little. I imagined if I could only find him enough horse quarters he might like me a lot. I never found enough.

Ben was a die-hard Calgary Flames fan, and as such, an equally passionate Edmonton Oilers hater. Trying to shun Wayne Gretzky in the 1980s was a difficult feat, but Ben Andersen made it look easy. He was a man of few passions, but hockey was one of them. *"Shoot! Shoot! Shoot you moron!"* he would shout at the TV as I sat by his feet attempting to look interested. *"No! No! No! Get it out of there you idiot!"* he would scream whenever the puck came near his goalie.

I hated hockey. It bored me to death. And though I found it hard to stay awake, I watched hockey with Ben because I thought if he believed I liked hockey he would like me. So I bought the T-shirt and the hat, memorized the names of the key players, talked about how much I hated the Oilers and declared this to be the year that *we*—the Flames—were sure to win the cup. It was, however, all an act. I couldn't care less if they won. The Flames were one thing to me, a way to spend time with Ben. I kept hoping one day he would see me screaming at the goalie, put his arm around me and say, "That's my boy!"

At age fourteen I saved enough money working at A&W to buy two tickets to a Calgary Flames alumni game where we could meet the players afterward. Lanny McDonald, Ben's favorite player, was going to be there. I saw this as a sure fire way to win Ben's heart. How could he *not* love me after giving him such a generous gift? I not only bought the tickets, I also bought Calgary Flames jerseys for both of us to wear to the game. Ben gladly accepted the offer and off to the game we went. We did meet the players and yes,

Lanny McDonald even signed our jerseys. Ben had a great time. It was obvious. As we drove home that evening I kept waiting for him to say something meaningful to me, anything to give me the impression I had done well, pleased him, and maybe even won a small place in his heart. Unfortunately, he didn't like hockey quite that much.

As children, if we ever heard "good job" or "well done," it came from mom. Encouragement wasn't Ben's forte. He pointed out what we did wrong, not what we did right. If I got 90% on a math test (it only happened once), he said, "Well, there's still room for improvement." It seemed he could find a flaw in anything. If it wasn't the way I did my chores, it was length of my hair, my report card, the way I dressed, slurped my soup, or the stupid question he assumed I ought to know the answer to. I always seemed to find a way to fail in my step-father's eyes.

I had said it a thousand times, "I love you dad", thinking one day he would respond, "I love you too," even if only because it was the appropriate response. Ben wasn't concerned about what was appropriate. His response was, "Okay." I once tried to pressure him into an "I love you" when I was about nine years old. He turned off my light at bedtime and as he was leaving the room I said, "Good night dad, I love you!" As he began to shut the door I added, "Hey dad! Doesn't that make you want to say something too?" He rolled his eyes and said, "Go to sleep!" My heart sunk as the door shut behind him. Was I really that hard to love?

Don't get me wrong. Ben Andersen was a good man, he really was, but he lived in prison. The few who knew him well called him *a gentle giant*. His bark was much worse than his bite and there was a sweetness hiding underneath all that thick skin. But boy was his skin thick! I spent decades trying to win him over but he was just too tough of a nut to crack.

My mom died of cancer when I was twenty-one, and Ben never remarried. He missed my mom and moped around like a beaten pup for years. Though he never gave me the impression he cared, I visited him from time to time, taking him for coffee, or to the occasional Flames game. When my wife and I were expecting our first child, the orphan inside of me still longing for a father's approval had an idea I was certain would penetrate even Ben Andersen's crusty old heart.

I had always liked the name Ben. Though he seemed like a grump, I loved Ben and I saw the good in him. Furthermore, my best friend in high school had the name Ben and I told him at age fourteen I was going to name my first son after him. He, in turn, promised to name his first son Steve (he didn't). It was a stupid teenage promise, the kind you just don't keep, but since he shared the same name as my step dad I saw an opportunity for sticking to my guns.

Throughout my wife's pregnancy I played the scenario over in my mind hundreds—literally hundreds—of times. My son would be born. Ben would come to visit the hospital. I would put the baby in his arms and eventually he would ask, "So, what did you name him?" At that moment I would look at him and casually say, "I named him after his grandfather. His name is Ben." And then I imagined my big burly step-dad looking at me, and with tears in his eyes he would say the words I had waited a lifetime to hear, "I love you son!" Then we would hug, and forever after our relationship would be different. I would have a place in his heart. I would be Steve Andersen—at least on the inside.

Well the day finally came. It was August 16, 2007, and my beautiful bride went into labor. It wasn't an easy birth and in the end the baby was delivered by C-section. I called my step-dad as soon as the baby was born and told him to come to the hospital and meet his first grandson. He arrived a few hours later and I could hardly contain my excitement. I had watched this moment play out in my mind over and over, but now I would see it unfold before my very eyes.

I said, "Here dad, you can hold him," as I handed him the little bundle.

Ben awkwardly received the baby, not quite sure how to hold him. He smiled and started making baby noises. "Red hair!" he said, "I sure wouldn't have expected that." After about a minute of making odd clicking noises and whistling bird noises as only Ben Andersen could do, he looked up and asked, "So, what did you name the little guy?"

It was the moment I had waited for all my life. On the inside my heart began to race, but on the outside I was as cool as a cucumber. As casually as I could manage I said, "Oh… I decided to name this one after his grandfather." Ben, not sure what that meant, tilted his head and said, "Huh? So what's his name?" I smiled and said, "His name is Ben."

Assuming I was trying to be funny and failing, my step-dad rolled his eyes and barked, "Don't be such a knuckle head! Really, what's his name?"

This time, more firmly, I said, "His name is Ben!"

Ben's eyes filled with tears, but rather than looking at me he quickly turned his attention back to the baby and locked onto little Ben like he was looking into a portal. He was mesmerized. I watched my step-father's lips and chin stiffen as he held back emotions he did not wish for me to see. He was speechless. Truly. Something was happening inside of him, that was plain to see, but what was it? I did not know. The gentle giant softly and lovingly bounced his first grandson in his arms for hours. The sparkle in his eyes and the smile on his face as he gazed at little Ben was a wonder to behold. All I could think was, *What I wouldn't do to have him look at me like that!*

He never thanked me for giving him a namesake. He never gave me the hug. He never called me his son, nor did he tell me I had honored him. And while I knew I had touched his heart, within weeks I found myself sitting across from him over a cup of coffee asking myself the same old questions. Does this guy even like me? Does he see any value in me? Is there any place in his heart for me? Will I ever be good enough?

By the time I was thirty-four years old I had preached around the world, written a book, married a magnificent woman, had two beautiful children and become a very wealthy in business, and yet in the eyes of my step-dad I still wondered if I had any value whatsoever. It didn't matter what I did, I just couldn't win with Ben Andersen. It took thirty-four years, but I finally gave up. I would never stop loving him or showing him kindness, but I determined to stop hoping to ever be loved back. It wasn't going to happen. I had done my best. I had tried everything.

Or had I?

Have You Done The Intercession?

One morning in 2010 at 5AM something dawned on me. I had been up all night preparing a sermon on the subject of spiritual prisons. Up until this time I had always illustrated the message with the story of Dennis' intercession for my biological father and the freedom I experienced as a result. I had not, however, put much thought into the impact my step-dad's relationship had on me. This particular morning, as I pondered the prayer of intercession, I began wondering if I had ever taken the time to do any intercession for Ben. Because I could not remember if I had, I took a few minutes to do it right then and there. It didn't take long. It was an unpassionate and calculated prayer. There were no tears. There was little emotion involved. More than anything, I was simply covering all the basis in my own life. I wanted to be certain I held no unforgiveness toward Ben Andersen as I knew it would hold me back in other ways.

The prayer went something like this:

Heavenly Father, I come to you in the name of Jesus Christ. I do not remember if I have done this before, and I apologize if I haven't. I want to intercede for my step-dad today. On his behalf I come to you and say, 'Please forgive me for the way I have withheld love from my step-son, Steve Holmstrom. He has always wanted my affection, and yet I have withheld it. Forgive me for not taking the time to walk with him, talk with him, to encourage and comfort him, and to be the father you wanted me to be to him. I'm so sorry I never threw a ball with him, put my arm around him, or told him how special he was. I'm sorry I never took him hunting or fishing or camping. I'm particularly sorry I have never once, in all these years, told him I loved him. Father, forgive me for my cold, cold heart. Please don't hold this sin against me, and if you would, please set me free from this spiritual prison which has held me hostage all my life.'"

Then I continued, "And I, Steve Holmstrom, declare today I completely forgive Ben Andersen for any sins he has committed against me. I realize it was hard for him to give what he himself never received from his parents. I hold no ill will toward

77

him, I cancel every debt he owes me and every I.O.U. As far as things are concerned with me, Ben Andersen is forgiven, and Lord I ask you to bless him in Jesus' name. Amen."

That was that. I had done the intercession for my step-dad. My words were spoken into the unseen realms and though it wasn't an emotional prayer, I meant it from my heart. What else could I do? Tired from staring at a computer screen all night, I decided to head to bed. It was 5:30 a.m.

Two and a half hours later, at 8 a.m., I was awoken by a phone call. It was my step dad calling for no reason at all. This was not unusual. He called from time to time, usually when he was missing the grandkids and hoping I would invite him to come for a visit. When he heard my groggy morning voice he said, "You're not still sleeping, are you? Get up you lazy bones! You know what the Bible says, don't you? *A little sleep, a little slumber, a little folding of the hands to rest, and then POVERTY will come upon you!*" I rolled my eyes and moaned as I always did whenever he quoted scripture to guilt me.

"Thanks Dad", I said with as much sarcasm as I could jam into two words, "It's just the verse I needed. But I was only sleeping because I was up until 5 a.m. working on a sermon!"

We talked for a few minutes about the usual stuff. I told him how the kids were doing, and he grumbled about little things that had annoyed him that week. His water bill was high. His back was sore. He had so much to do and so little time, which we both knew was a lie. Truthfully, he was bored sick of retirement, and had even asked his former employer to take him back two days a week just to get out of the house. Finally, I asked him when he was going to come and visit the kids. He acted like it was a burden, but then said, "Well, I suppose I could come that way tomorrow, but only for a night or two, and only if you *really* want me to." I insisted I did, which was not completely true, but it was what he wanted to hear.

Before I hung up the phone to attempt to go back to sleep, I thanked him for calling and said the same four words I ended all our phone calls with. I had said them thousand times, "I love you dad". This time, however, something different happened. Something I was not expecting. Something I had done nothing to earn. I will never forget that glorious moment. He said it quietly, he said it quickly, and it didn't sound all that natural, but I distinctly heard the words, "I love you too". And with a click, he was gone.

Well that woke me up! All I could think was, *What? How? Now? Why?* And then it struck me… the intercession! I had *just* done the intercession! I confessed his sin to God on his behalf, sincerely forgave him, and in less than three hours my step-dad spoke the words I waited my entire life to hear! All I could do was sit there on the side of my bed and cry. I wanted so badly to call him back and ask him to say it one more time, but a little slower.

He came for a visit and stayed a few days. He wasn't exactly warm and fuzzy, but he did seem different. And then, as he was leaving, it happened again! I told him I loved him and his response as he was walking out the door was, "I love you too… and you need to mow your lawn kid!"

Ben Andersen lived two more years before unexpectedly dying of a brain aneurism. Before he died, however, I heard those beautiful words at least one hundred more times. Never did he fail, on any phone call or visit, to speak those words to me. He even started saying it a little slower. I had always hugged him, whether he liked it or not, but in his last two years he began to hug me back. In his own gruff-quiet-bashful-way he offered me more love in those two years than he had in the previous thirty years combined. I had always hoped he had room in his heart for me, but was never sure. It turned out he did. I was his son, he loved me, and I even have his horse quarters to prove it.

I had always imagined Ben's affection was something he withheld because he chose to. I do not see it that way any longer. Like many, he lived his life in a prison. He had no choice. By the grace and mercy of God, a simple prayer of intercession unlocked his prison and within two and a half hours that big bear of a man left his cage and came out for a visit. He was never the same again.

Don't spend your life attempting to unlock a prison with the wrong key. Do the intercession.

Repented on their behalf. Forgiven them, release them, and tear up every I.O.U. While you cannot force anyone to leave their prison, you can use the key of intercession to unlock it.

FIVE

Intercession in Business

While the prayer of intercession is a marvellous ministry tool, it is not to be reserved for altar calls and prayer rooms. It is as useful to the teacher, the lawyer, the plumber and the politician as it is to the church leader. I have found it to be particularly helpful in running a successful business. In fact, I have seen greater financial breakthroughs as a result of intercessory prayer than any other type of prayer. Why? Because most business problems are people problems and most people problems can be helped and often solved through intercession.

The salesman living in a spiritual prison is less effective connecting with customers than the one who isn't. You could spend thousands of dollars sending him to the best sales workshops in the country, but they will never free him from a spiritual prison. First partner with the Holy Spirit through intercession and watch what God can do. Unlock his prison. His whole life will be blessed as a result, including his benefit to your business.

Do you have a staff member whose broken marriage has left her downcast and despondent? It's hard to get high productivity out of someone who cannot lift their head. She may benefit from both vertical intercession (repenting to God on her or her husband's behalf) and horizontal intercession (repenting to her on behalf of her husband). Do the intercession and watch God bring something beautiful out of something ugly. It might even save their marriage.

Most business problems are people problems and most people problems can be helped and often solved through intercession

Do you have a customer whose fear and lack of trust keep you from landing a deal? I cannot say it enough. *Do the intercession! Do the intercession! Do the intercession!* Intercession will change things. When you see the results of intercession for yourself, you will be sold. It works. While the wages of sin is death to businesses, friendships, marriages, churches and destinies, intercession is often the solution. It opens the door to the grace of God while shutting the door to the enemy produced by unrepented sin.

A few months ago I found myself stewing over a competitor of mine in the oil patch. Let's call him "Troy". It wasn't that Troy was stealing my customers (although he did try and fail), what bothered me was how much he seemed to detest me. I'll confess I like to be liked. I try to treat people with kindness, even competitors, because I want to get along with everyone I can. Unfortunately, no matter how kind I was to Troy, he seemed to hate me more and more. He talked down about me to my customers. He ignored me when I said hello. On the odd occasion where he did look my way, it was with an air of superiority that just makes a redneck like me want to punch a guy in the mouth.

For a little while it didn't bother me much. I knew he was jealous and I understood why. The favor of God on my life caused my company to grow even when others didn't. I had compassion on Troy. Favor isn't fair. When I heard he was snubbing and talking down to a few of my staff, however, my compassion began to dwindle.

One day, as I was venting my frustration to my wife, she oh-so-lovingly (not really) pointed out my lack of love for Troy. She figured I needed to change my attitude toward him. I, of course, justified myself and she called me out on that as well. Finally she said, *"Honey, have you done the intercession for Troy?"* Of course the answer was no. With a little more encouragement from my wife, I finally conceded to put on his gabi.

I knew Troy wasn't going to repent on his own, and if I suggested he did, he'd likely spit in my face. Any confession of sin would have to come from my mouth, not his. So right there in my living room with my wife at my side, I stood in the gap for Troy and repented on his behalf.

Ironically, or not so ironically, I bumped into Troy the very next week at the playground. I had taken my kids there, and he had taken his. This time, however,

Troy didn't shun me. When I called his name and said hello, he looked right at me, smiled as though he was genuinely pleased to see me and then walked over and started a conversation. We chatted like old friends for about fifteen minutes. All I could think was, *I can't believe it worked!* I almost started to like the guy. Almost.

Where there are unconfessed sins there are always going to be issues. Convincing someone else to repent of their sins can be difficult or impossible. Putting on their gabi and doing it for them is not difficult at all.

Big Bad Joe

In 2012 I had a very good customer named Joe (not his real name). When I say Joe was a good customer, I do not mean he was a good person. Joe was anything but good. He had a reputation for gross immorality, drug abuse, drunkenness, promiscuous sex and bribery. He took pleasure in, and even boasted about, his talent for making people feel worthless. Being over six and a half feet tall only added to his ability to make others feel small. Joe was hated by almost everyone who worked with him, but many feared him because he had enormous influence in the oil patch. If he liked you, you could make a lot of money. He liked me a lot, and as a result he gave my company over a million dollars' worth of work each year. That is what made Joe a "good" customer.

People wondered, and often asked me, why Joe threw me so much work. Some believed I bribed him with kickbacks, while others assumed he was a silent partner in our company. No one, however, knew the truth. It was too outrageous to cross anyone's mind. The truth—if you can believe it—was that big mean terrible Joe actually had a hunger for God. He liked me because I was a preacher and he watched Oilpatch Pulpit.

Joe had had an unusual encounter with the Holy Spirit years earlier which shook him to the core. As a result of this experience he put his faith in Christ. He wasn't living as immorally as he once had, but still had the reputation of a dirt bag and a bad habit of treating people like garbage. Now, a secret believer with plenty of rough edges to camouflage his faith, Joe had been watching my sermon videos on oilpatchpulpit.com.

My relationship with Joe was much like David's early relationship with Saul. Just as Saul kept David close to gain relief from his demons, Joe seemed to keep me around for the same reason. He battled with incredible spiritual oppression which manifested in different ways.

On numerous occasions I entered his oilfield shack only to find him moaning in pain, laying on his couch holding his head. I'd say, "Hey Joe, what's going on?" He'd lament about the pain, or the strange cloudiness that kept him from thinking straight. I would say, "You know it's just a demon, right? A small one, about the size of a cat. You just need to learn to shoo them away." He never wanted to learn. He always asked me to do it for him. So I would speak to the demon, command it to leave, and within minutes

Joe would be back on his feet, grinning, painless, clear headed, and thanking me. He seemed to think it was a magic trick or something.

From time to time Joe would call asking me to come out to his lease and B.S. with him. B.S. was our code for *Bible study*. I would drive out to where he was working in the patch, sometimes hours away, just to spend a half an hour teaching Joe the Word. I tried to give him keys to be a better husband, father, and boss. I pleaded with him to turn from immorality and embrace a pure and holy life. I talked to him about kindness, love, and mercy. Unfortunately, it didn't take. Like many today, Joe wanted a kingdom life but wasn't willing to pay the price. I couldn't even get him to read his Bible regularly or memorize a single scripture. Spiritually, he was a baby, always needing to be propped up and spoon fed. Eventually my patience began to wear thin.

After working with Joe for several years, I lost all his work overnight. A beautiful saleswoman employed by one of my competitors paid him a visit and she ended up offering him a little more than oilfield equipment. When he started sleeping with her she immediately landed all his work. I tried to talk to him but he became defensive, made excuses, and told me it wasn't what I thought. His staff, however, told me it was exactly what I thought. With colorful metaphors they explained to me that as long as Joe was having sex with my competition, I wouldn't be getting any more of their business.

I was sick about losing the work, it was a lot of money, and I was heartbroken for Joe as well. As much as his shallow walk had frustrated me, he was a friend. We had spent a lot of time together. I cared about him. His inability to say no to the flesh was costing me a friend, his wife a husband, and his kids were hurting too. Joe dumped his wife and starting calling the saleswoman his girlfriend. Oh how I wanted to lay hands on him!

On the Day of Atonement the following year, while fasting and praying before the Lord, I slipped into a vision. In the vision I saw Satan holding what seemed to be three monstrous-like dogs on leashes. Above the dogs I saw a sign which read *PD 101*, and I knew it stood for *The School of Poverty and Disease*. With ferocious eyes fixed on Joe, the dogs pulled hard against their leashes. They wanted to kill him. Then I saw the Lord with His hand held open toward the devil, as if to say, "WAIT!" The enemy did not have permission to release those monsters on Joe, at least not yet. In the vision, I knew Jesus was giving Joe a window of time to repent.

Then the scene changed and I saw Joe in a hospital bed, sick, depressed, and all alone. He had lost everything, his job, his health, his influence, his money and his family. I then saw myself entering the hospital room to visit and pray for Joe. The vision ended and just as it did I heard the voice of the Lord say to me, *"Your friend Joe has chosen the way of Herod and I am preparing my judgment against him."*

Later that day I shared the vision with my wife and Dennis and Katie. We knew we had to intercede for Joe. I stood in the gap for Joe and repented on his behalf. My wife stood in the gap for the saleswoman and repented for her part in all of it. We asked the Lord to be merciful and to set them free from their sins.

> **Intercession will unlock a person's prison, but it does not force them to walk out of it**

I would like to say Joe called the next day with a change of heart, but that's not how the story ends. Intercession cannot control another person. That would be witchcraft. Intercession will unlock a person's prison, but it does not force them to leave it, and some don't want to. As they say, you can lead a horse to water but you cannot make him drink.

I called Joe a few days later to try to talk to him but he was unwilling to budge. I begged him to turn from his adulterous relationship, but he said, "You're just saying all this to get my work back. It's all about money for you. You're being selfish!" The money certainly had crossed my mind, but it wasn't the only reason for my call. I genuinely feared for Joe's life. I cared about his broken marriage. I cared about his three teenage daughters who now despised him. I cared about his soul.

I said, "Joe, I had a vision last week and I saw three large demons Satan plans to loose on you. They will manifest as poverty and disease. If you do not repent, and quick, you are in big trouble. These are not like the little kittens I've chased out of your shack. These dogs aren't coming to give you a headache, they're coming to destroy your life. Mark my word, if you don't change direction fast I'll be visiting you in a hospital. I've already seen it. You will lose everything, including your health. The Lord told me, *Your friend Joe has chosen the way of Herod and I am preparing my judgment against him.* Joe, you are my friend and I love you. You need to trust me now. This is serious!" Knowing Joe had no clue what happened to Herod, I quoted to him Acts 12:21-23, which says:

> *On an appointed day Herod, having put on his royal apparel, took his seat on the rostrum and began delivering an address to them. The people kept crying out, "The voice of a god and not of a man!" And immediately an angel of the Lord struck him because he did not give God the glory, and he was eaten by worms and died.*

Well that was all Joe wanted to hear. He insisted I was inventing visions to manipulate him into getting his work back and then Joe hung up the phone. He then sent two members of the Hell's Angels motorcycle club to pay me a visit. They threatened me, telling me not to contact Joe, his family, his new girlfriend, or anyone connected to him. I thanked them for their visit, gave them Oilpatch Pulpit hardhat stickers, and told them if their organization ever needed a chaplain I would be honored to serve them for free. They didn't seem interested. When the bikers left I figured it might be best to stop calling Joe. He obviously didn't want to B.S. with me anymore.

Over the next few months Joe's life began to spiral. His stress level soared as he was hit from every direction. He had troubles at work, an angry wife with a talent for revenge, three furious teenage daughters who now considered him a devil, a guilty conscience, and escalating health problems. His life was in a freefall. Everything that could go wrong, did go wrong. In a drunken moment of depression and desperation Joe swallowed a bottle of pills in an attempt to end his life. Before he fell asleep, however, he texted a picture of the empty pill bottle to a friend, who called the ambulance.

Because of his attempted suicide, Joe was admitted to a psych ward of a hospital and was not allowed to leave for weeks. That, of course, kept him from going to work, and before long half the oil patch had heard the rumours. News spread fast. Before he left the hospital he had lost his job, his influence, his reputation, his girlfriend and his family. He lost everything.

I went to visit Joe in the hospital. It was awkward, to say the least. I watched him take his meds and couldn't believe how many different pills they had him on. He explained to me all the different troubles he was having with his body and what each pill was meant to accomplish. It was sad to see my friend in such rough shape. In a moment of honesty and hopelessness, Joe looked at me and said, "Steve, you were right. Everything you said would happen, happened. I lost everything. My life is over."

I prayed for Joe and tried to encourage him, but we both knew the road ahead was going to be difficult. It's not easy being a wealthy and influential oilfield boss one day and having to start over with an atrocious reputation the next. It's worse than starting from scratch. God wasn't kidding when He said *"The way of a transgressor is hard"*. It is.

Not long after seeing Joe, my wife and I visited with Dennis and Katie in their home. The four of us took an hour to do some more intercession surrounding the whole situation. We interceded for Joe and his girlfriend again, covering some of the same bases and a few more. We interceded on behalf of the companies involved, including the competitor company which landed all Joe's work. I repented for myself and sins I committed in the process, and forgave Joe and my competitor once again.

My wife and I hadn't finished driving home from Dennis and Katie's house that day when I received a text message from Joe's old boss. All the message said was, "We need to get together and talk about work". As it turned out, my competitor had been overcharging but Joe had let it slide, perhaps to make his new girlfriend happy. Now that Joe was out, so was my competitor. We got all the work back. All the new boss wanted was honesty, hard work, and a fair price. There would be no more B.S. (the other kind).

I will say it again, just in case you forgot to underline it the first time. *Most business problems are people problems and most people problems can be helped, and often solved, through intercession.* Take intercession to work and see what God will do.

SIX

Revival Belongs to the Intercessors

There is a lot of talk about revival these days. To many, it would seem, revival is just around the corner and only a matter of time. "Look how dark it's getting," they say, "Things couldn't get much worse, so the Lord must be about to release His glory." This sort of superficial optimism leads to deferred hope and sick hearts. You would be surprised how much worse things could get.

Revival does not come "when it's time". It is an *effect* which follows a very specific *cause*. Every true outpouring of glory and power has come as a result of a group of moaning, groaning, travailing, birthing intercessors. Whether it be a national revival, a city revival, a local church revival, or just the revival of your own cold heart, pull back the curtain and you'll find someone standing in the gap. Revival belongs to the intercessors.

For a long time the enemy convinced the church intercession was only for a few grey-haired women. While I'm grateful for our elder-sister-warriors who have met in back rooms contending for the little glory we have known, they must not carry this burden alone. Ladies, we're coming to help, and we are coming by the thousands!

God is equipping men and women, young and old, to stand in the gap as intercessors. Just last weekend I taught a thirty-seven year old businessman named Jesse about intercession and within minutes I watched this fellow go into full out intercessory travail on the floor like he was a woman in labor. I didn't know whether I should call an ambulance or a doula. I was like, "Jesse, are you sure you haven't done this before? I didn't even teach you that part. You do this like the old-gals do!"

I am of the opinion a mighty revival *is* at our doorstep, but not because it's been "so long" since the last one and so "it must be time". I believe it because I see the intercessors arising! I see the firewall being built and the generations taking their place. People who have never felt compelled to pray are finding their way to the prayer room. Once beautifully round and well fed faces are now skinny from fasting. Those who thought they could never cry are falling on their faces and weeping in agony. There is a wave of intercession arising and spreading across the nations of the earth. Do not miss the wave! It doesn't matter if you're sixteen or ninety-six, male or female, red, yellow, black or white. You are called to intercession. Join us! We need your help. There will be no end time revival, no billion soul harvest, and no outpouring of glory and power without a multitude of intercessors crying out in agony, *"God forgive us! God save us! God heal our land!"*

The Kingdom of Priests

The *King James Version* did the church a great disservice in its interpretation of Revelation 1:6 and 5:10. It uses the phrase *"kings and priests"* when it should read *"kingdom of priests" or "kingdom and priests."* This is error because in Greek, just as in English, the words *king* and *kingdom* have completely different meanings. Being part of a kingdom does not make you a king. As a result of this error in translation, there has been a lot of teaching on the subject of *"kings and priests"*. Worse yet, even though the *King James Version* refers to kings *and* priests, many have pushed this even further by inferring the idea of kings *or* priests.

Let me explain why this is significant. The usual implication of this popular teaching is that you are either one or the other. Pastors and church leaders are referred to as *priests*, while those in business or high places of influence are considered *kings*. Other folks aren't sure where they fit. Many businesspeople enjoy this train of thought as it gives them an upper hand over the pastors and spiritual leaders in their lives. No one tells a king what to do!

It's malarkey. Jesus *has made us to be a kingdom, priests to His God and Father* (Rev. 1:6), and as a result we will *reign upon the earth* (Rev. 5:10). We are all priests, a whole kingdom of priests, yet priest who reign! Even if you embrace the idea of believers as kings on the earth (and I believe it is thin ice), it is never kings *or* priests. It is not one or the other. We are all priests.

A priest is an intercessor, one who has been granted access to the very throne of God to offer praise, thanksgiving and worship, and one who stands in the gap on behalf of others. In the Old Testament only the Levites, just one tribe out of the twelve, had the privilege of access to the presence of God. The church today, however, is a whole *kingdom of priests!* We all have access. Every believer has been given the priestly ministry of intercession. It is a greater calling than that of a king. Kings were not permitted in the Holy of Holies. You have to be a priest to enter in.

In my nation of Canada I have joined with intercessors across the country in gatherings we have referred to as the *Battle for Canada*. While the gatherings certainly include much high praise and worship, intercession is at the heart of it all. For days, even up to ten, we have gathered en masse crying out and repenting to God for the sins of our nation (vertical intercession). We have repented to men, women, and people groups on behalf of those who have exploited, oppressed, and misused them (horizontal intercession). I have watched thousands weep over the bloodshed of millions of unborn children, the atrocities committed against our First

> **As intercessors, we are not finished until we are finished and we know we are finished when God heals our land!**

Nations people, and the division between the French and the English. We have repented for the church's rejection of apostolic and prophetic ministries, and for the sexual perversion and immorality of our day. We do not gather to hear popular speakers or big bands. We do not gather to be entertained. We gather to wrap ourselves in the dirty gabis of our generation and to cry out for mercy, healing and deliverance in our nation.

Many times we have had critics say, "We've already done the repentance for that. Why are you repenting to the Natives again? Why the French? Why are you still banging on the abortion drum? That's already been dealt with, so why rehash old issues?"

If it has already been dealt with, where is the healing? Where is the transformation? Where is the revival of hearts and souls? Where is the glory and power we have been promised? As intercessors, we are not finished until we are finished and we know we are finished *when God heals our land!* We know we are finished when local churches cannot contain the millions of souls being saved in our stadium gatherings. We know we are finished when blind eyes open, when deaf ears hear, when the dead are raised, and when our children are no longer murdered in their mother's wombs. We know we are finished when the church is doing what Jesus said she would do.

Until that day, we need intercessors. We need priests. A whole kingdom of them! Will you join us? Will you gather with us? Rather than grumbling about your miserable drunk uncle, will you stand in the gap and repent on his behalf? Will you repent on behalf of your family, your church, your city, and your nation? Will you gather with other intercessors in small groups and large groups, in living rooms and chat rooms, in open fields and stadiums and who knows where else? Will you help us raise up a cry that cannot be ignored?

> *If My people, who are called by My name, will humble themselves and pray and seek My face and turn from their wicked ways, then I will hear from heaven, and I will forgive their sin and will heal their land* (2 Chron. 7:14 NIV)

God is looking for intercessors. Without their repentance, destruction is immanent.

> *I searched for a man among them who would build up the wall and stand in the gap before Me for the land, so that I would not destroy it; but I found no one* (Ezekiel 22:30)

Our land is being destroyed for lack of intercession. Don't leave it to the grey-hairs. They cannot do this without us. Abraham interceded for Sodom alone, and where is that twisted city today? It will take a colossal wave of intercession to release a colossal wave of revival. You may feel like your little prayers are just a drop in the bucket, but every wave is made of a million drops. I write these words on my hands and knees. I'm begging you. PLEASE JOIN US! We need your equity! We need your voice! We need you to take your place in this kingdom of priests, to stand in the gap, to join the firewall, to wrap yourself in a filthy gabi, to moan, to groan, and to birth with us something new upon the earth!

I have a feeling, however, you are already on board. You wouldn't have read this far if you weren't. Thank you. On behalf of a world in desperate need of revival, I thank you from the bottom of my heart. We are going to see a great awakening and you are going to be part of the reason why.

Before I let you go I want to leave you with three very important pieces of advice.

1. Go With The Flow

While preparing this book I asked Katie if she had any suggestions for me. She said, *"Steve, just make sure you give them a model, not a formula. People tend to think if they don't get the words just right the prayer will not work. It isn't like that. People need to catch the spirit of intercession, not just our particular method. They don't have to say it like we say it. Help them to find their own way."* I hope I have done that for you in this book.

When I put on Dowit's gabi I wasn't thinking about how a prayer of intercession is supposed to sound, I was drinking a cup and going with the flow. The Holy Spirit took over and by the time I was done I felt like a woman who just gave birth. I had no clue what travail was. Dennis and Katie hadn't taught me about that yet. The whole situation was completely unplanned, uncomfortable, and unbelievably weird—yet it worked.

As you enter into the intercessory assignments the Lord places upon you, the best advice I can give you is to *go with the flow!* Don't worry about saying everything just right and don't worry about making mistakes. Forget the script and let the Holy Spirit lead you. He is big enough to tell you when you are missing it. If you surround yourself with seasoned intercessors they too will rein you in when necessary, but you have to give yourself the freedom to get lost in the current of the moment. Most assignments will not play out exactly as you would predict. The Holy Spirit is leading and rarely does what you think He's going to do.

The wind blows where it wishes and you hear the sound of it, but do not know where it comes from and where it is going; so is everyone who is born of the Spirit (John 3:8).

2. Follow the Burden

Maybe you're saying, "Alright, I'm in, but where do I start?" Start by following the burdens of your heart. Don't intercede for your nation until you have a burden for your nation. Begin with what matters to you. If God has given you a burden for just one person, perhaps your spouse or a friend from work, start there. Intercession is a gift you can give to your children, your parents, your siblings, your friends, or anyone you carry in your heart. Start by interceding for those you love.

If God gives you a burden for your town or city, gather with likeminded intercessors and raise up a cry for your region. Be faithful with the assignments He gives you, as small as they may seem, and He will trust you with more. God may one day place a particular nation or people group in your heart. For now, however, only intercede for things that weigh on your heart. Follow the burden.

3. Bind Retaliation

Whenever you engage in intercession (and I have learned this the hard way) be sure to *bind all retaliation from the enemy* afterward. Satan loses power in the lives of those you intercede for, and given the opportunity he will gladly kick you in the teeth as a thank you for your ministry. He will retaliate if you leave an open door for him to do so. So don't. Shut the door to retaliation. It doesn't take long. It is a simple prayer and it always seems to work. I usually pray something like this:

> *Father I thank you for the breakthrough which has been accomplished through this intercession, I know it will bear great fruit! In the Name of Jesus Christ I now draw a bloodline of protection around my life, my wife, my children, our businesses, our finances, our health, our ministry, our extended family and anything pertaining to us. I declare that there will be NO RETALIATION from the enemy and that no weapon formed against us will prosper! Thank You for your protection Lord.*

One little prayer like that one may just save you a dent in bumper or leak in your roof. Seriously. Always bind retaliation. You'll thank me later.

We love hearing the stories of brand new intercessors. If you have a story you would like to share with us, be sure to send us an e-mail to *feedback@oilpatchpulpit.com*. We would love to hear from you. Some of the greatest results often come through newbie intercessors who have no clue what they are doing. One last story about such a person, and then I'll let you go…

My Mother's a Witch

A number of years ago I was invited to preach a week of meetings at a church in St. John, Newfoundland. The first few days went great and were well received by all. On the Saturday night, however, I spoke on the subject of intercession and things didn't go so well. The pastor who had invited me was visibly struggling with my message as I preached. Perhaps I wasn't explaining it well. In any case, just as I was finishing my message and about to invite people to come forward for ministry, he walked up on stage. The pastor took the microphone from me and said, *"Church, I just feel the Holy Spirit saying we need to take a few minutes right now to pray in the Spirit!"* He then took the meeting in a completely different direction. I had been hoping to lead people into prayers of intercession for their family members, and into prayers of forgiveness as well. I knew there were many spiritual prisons needing to be unlocked.

The next morning, during which I was scheduled to preach, the pastor "felt led" once again to have an extended time of praying in the spirit during worship and as a result there just happened to be no time for a sermon. My last scheduled meeting was the Sunday night service, but surprise, surprise, the Lord had another plan.

After the Sunday night service a woman in her mid-fifties approached me. She wanted to tell me how much my message on intercession had meant to her. I was shocked. I hadn't even finished that sermon. It was the message which had killed my week of meetings. She said, "Last night, when our pastor shut you down," (apparently it was obvious,) "I knew where you were going, so I went there anyway. I knew I needed to intercede for and forgive some family members of mine. After the meeting I drove straight to the graveyard!" This was getting interesting.

She continued, "My grandfather sexually molested me all through my childhood and I've hated him my entire life. But last night I went to his grave, laid down right on top of it and repented on his behalf. Then I bawled my eyes out and I told my grandpa, 'Grandpa, I forgive you! I release you! I cancel every debt you owe me and I tear up every I.O.U. You don't owe me anything anymore. You're forgiven!'" I knew I had said nothing in my sermon about talking to the dead, but awkwardly smiled and said, "Oh, how wonderful sister."

She continued, "Then I went home and started thinking about my mom. You see, my mother is a witch." When I told her she probably shouldn't say such a mean thing about her mom, she insisted, "No, literally! She is actually a witch. From the time I was little she has only wore black and she's involved in every kind of witchcraft imaginable. She casts spells on people and everything, and it works. Years ago, when my sister got cancer, I knew in my heart my mother was behind it. She had opened a dark door and it was killing my sister. I begged my mother to turn from her witchcraft, but she wouldn't. My sister died and I have hated my mother ever since."

"But last night,", she continued, "after I got home from the graveyard, I decided to intercede for my mom as well. I stood in the gap for her and repented for all the witchcraft she has been involved in. After that I spent some time ripping up I.O.U.s. I even forgave her for killing my sister."

At this point the woman broke down weeping. When she regained her composure she said, "Well, I never told my mother anything about last night's intercession or how I forgave her. I haven't talked to her in years and she lives on the other side of Newfoundland. But after this morning's service I received a phone call from my mom! She was calling to ask me if I would take her shopping for new clothes.

When I asked her why, she said she woke up this morning with a strange desire to go to church!"

The woman then threw her hands in the air for dramatic effect and said, "Steven! Did you hear me? She woke up this morning feeling like going to CHURCH! My mother NEVER feels like going to church! But today she got up, went to church, heard the gospel, and she gave her life to Jesus Christ! My mother, *the witch*, said, 'Can you be a darling and take me shopping for some new clothes? All I have is black and I don't want to look like a witch anymore.'"

The woman then dropped her head on my shoulder and wept again, thanking me for teaching her the prayer of intercession. Her mother, once bound for decades, was immediately set free by a merciful God responding to a baby intercessor's simple prayer. What a wonder intersession is! So much power to set prisoners free, yet so easily attainable to any and all who will join this royal priesthood, this kingdom of priests.

It's Your Turn

For over twenty years I have been telling the world about a man named Dennis who, through a simple act of intercession, unlocked my prison and set me free. You wouldn't be reading these words if he hadn't. Since that time I have seen countless miracles in my life and in the lives of others through this simple prayer. Intercession has become so much a part of our daily lives that, when frustrated about anything, my wife and I regularly ask each other, "Did you do the intercession?" The answer is almost always no, because when we've done the intercession we rarely experience frustration. Do the intercession and you will see the same results. I guarantee it.

But now it is time to act. No more reading. It is time to embrace the call to intercession! Only God knows what chains will be broken, what prisons unlocked, and what adventures await you as you stand in the gap on behalf of others. I just have one question for you. Who will be your next Dowit?

Do You Know Jesus?

If you are not serving the Lord Jesus right now, yet you read books like this, you are one hungry soul! What is stopping you? Jesus is Lord of the universe, your designer and creator, and He loves you more than you have ever loved anything or anyone. He knows you're a mess, yet He *still* wants you to be a part of His forever family. Don't wait another day, begin your journey with Jesus today!

Some put Jesus off for as long as they think they can. They say, "I'll give my life to Christ when I'm really old, when my life is done and I've had my fun." It doesn't work like that. Jesus said, *"No one can come to Me unless the Father who sent Me draws him"* (John 6:44). You don't get to pick the day you say yes to Jesus. The time to respond is the moment the Father tugs on your heart. Is that not today?

Others put Jesus off because they believe a lie. Some believe a person must "clean his life up first", or that they have gone too far, waited too long. But that's not true. If you are still breathing, it isn't too late, and only Jesus can clean you up. That's His specialty!

Don't let the devil smooth talk you into hell. His reasoning may make sense from a human perspective, but if you believe him you will regret it forever. Resist the devil, say yes to Jesus while His arms are open wide, and begin living for Him today. You're never going to be perfect, but you can start walking with the One who is right now.

God loves you very much and He has made a way for you to receive eternal life, but only one, and it is through faith in His Son. If you know you need to get right with God, please pray this prayer out loud, and from your heart:

Dear Heavenly Father, it's me _____, and I know it's time to get right with You. I'm sorry I have waited so long.

I admit I am a sinner. I have messed up, I have hurt people, I have hurt myself, and I have broken Your heart. Please forgive me.

I believe in Your Son, Jesus Christ. I believe He died on a cross as punishment for my sins so I wouldn't have to be punished. He paid my penalty as a gift to me, and I receive that gift today. I didn't earn it, I don't deserve it, but I thank You for it.

Jesus, I confess that You are Lord of all and today I commit my life to You. Please come and live in me. Teach me to hear the voice of Your Spirit and to follow You. Help me to live for You and to become all You dreamed I would be when You first thought me up. May Your Kingdom come and Your will be done in my life.

Thank You for loving me, forgiving me, calling me, and even noticing me! Anoint my heart to love You well. In Jesus Name, amen.

If you prayed that prayer, and truly meant it, your sins have been forgiven and you can begin calling God your Father. You can even call Him "Dad" if you like! He loves you and has not only given you eternal life, but a whole kingdom you may now begin to pursue and explore!

Pray regularly, meditate on the Word, gather and worship with other believers, and keep reading books and listening to messages which sow into your spiritual life. If you enjoyed this book, check out *oilpatchpulpit.com* and you will find plenty more to chew on, most of which is free. If you gave your life to Christ, I would love to hear from you. E-mail me a hello to feedback@oilpatchpulpit.com.

God bless you friend. I wish you the kingdom!

FOR INFORMATION ABOUT STEVE
HOLMSTROM'S BOOKS, MINISTRY, ITINERARY,
OR TO ACCESS HIS FREE VIDEO LIBRARY, VISIT:

OILPATCHPULPIT.COM

NOTES

Manufactured by Amazon.ca
Bolton, ON